W9-BGV-020

The Exquisite Life
of Oscar Wilde

The
EXQUISITE LIFE
of
Oscar Wilde

STEPHEN CALLOWAY
& DAVID COLVIN

ORION

First published in 1997 by ORION MEDIA
This paperback edition published in 1999 by ORION
An imprint of ORION BOOKS LTD
Orion House 5 Upper St Martin's Lane London WC2H 9EA

TITLE PAGE: Oscar Wilde in New York, 1882,
at the beginning of his 'long and lovely suicide'.

COVER PHOTOGRAPHS:
BACK: Bord Faílte/Irish Tourist Board, Dublin
FRONT: Weidenfeld Archive

Designed by
THE BRIDGEWATER BOOK COMPANY
Litho origination by
PIXEL COLOUR LTD, LONDON
Printed and bound in Great Britain by
BUTLER & TANNER LTD, FROME & LONDON

British Library Cataloguing in Publication data available

CONTENTS

Those Whom the Gods Love Grow Young

WHEN OSCAR WILDE DIED *in 1900, his funeral was not the elaborate interment that he might a few short years before have expected, but an altogether more sober affair. His very name had been anathema for almost six years, and it was not into the extraordinary Jacob Epstein mausoleum at Père Lachaise that his body was placed, but a mere mortal's grave, in a suburban Parisian cemetery, its site marked by a simple slab.*

Lonely and impoverished, he had died in a hired room in a Paris hotel after a career of almost unparalleled success, followed by disgrace, imprisonment and a continental exile of three years, during which his mental decline had been almost as marked as his physical. After his trials and imprisonment, his friends in society had for the most part deserted him; at the burial ceremony those who remained were almost outnumbered by journalists.

Under Queen Victoria the arts were at last receiving some measure of recognition; certain artists were accorded an unprecedented measure of adulation. Oscar Wilde might have hoped, by the age of

Oscar Wilde in the famous bottle-green overcoat. 'It has been all over America with me. It was at all my first nights. It knows me perfectly.'

forty-five, to have won for himself some of the honours – if not the baronies bestowed on a Leighton or a Tennyson - that were so freely given to other artists of his age. No such laurels would garland his brow.

For ten years his grave remained, seemingly forgotten, at Bagneux. Wilde's remaining friends were not rich, and his name was still controversial. Even to voice a qualified admiration for an artist more reviled than even Byron had been in his time was, as far as Victorian society was concerned, tantamount to countenancing the crimes which it had found so revolting that it had demanded the poet's utter destruction as atonement for them.

The erection of the Epstein tomb, however, marked the turning point in the fortune of his reputation. Robbie Ross, his literary executor and most loyal friend, spent the ten years after Wilde's death rescuing and rebuilding his reputation from the oblivion into which a moment's madness had cast it.

To the dinner at which the tomb's commission was announced came over two hundred of the great and good subjects of King Edward VII, prepared publicly to announce their regard for the once disgraced poet. By the 1940s, visitors to Wilde's tomb ten times outnumbered those to the graves of Chopin, Balzac, and all the other revered figures interred at Père Lachaise. The place of Oscar Wilde in the pantheon of English letters was finally assured.

RIGHT: Wilde at Oxford in 1878. 'I know I have a first,'
he boasted to his less brilliant colleagues; 'It's all a bore.'

CHAPTER ONE

Looking at the Stars

O SCAR WILDE'S DUBLIN *beginnings were unusual enough to portend something out of the common run of men. William Wilde, his father, was a pioneering and well-known doctor who, in addition to writing seminal textbooks in the new field of ocular medicine, and holding the position of Surgeon-Oculist to the Queen, was a distinguished archæologist, and the author of volumes on travel, history and biography.*

William Wilde's reputation as a scholar of Irish folklore attracted the attention of a young Irish poet and incendiary called Jane Elgee. Jane, who romantically but mistakenly believed herself to be descended from Dante, had adopted the *nom de plume*, or rather *nom de guerre* of 'Speranza', under which she penned spirited verses on lofty themes. In a literary attempt to rouse the Irish nation to overthrow its English oppressors in 1849, she had very nearly gone to prison for seditious libel, and she

ABOVE: *A caricature of Sir William Wilde and his colourful wife. 'Children begin by loving their parents. After a time they judge them. Rarely, if ever, do they forgive them.'*

LEFT: *Dublin in the nineteenth century. Oscar used to say that the Irish were a nation of brilliant failures, but the greatest talkers since the Greeks.*

Perhaps the earliest photograph of Oscar Wilde. 'The child is father of the man.' Nineteenth-century superstition led many mothers to put their infant sons in girls' clothes.

remained a romantic revolutionary in the grandest theatrical manner. She and William had married in 1851, and produced three children: William Robert Kingsbury Wills, in 1852; Oscar Fingal O'Flahertie Wills, born on 16 October 1854, and Isola, the only girl, with only one name, in 1857.

In addition to the range of his philanthropic and public activities, William Wilde's private affairs were prodigiously fraught. He acknowledged three illegitimate children in Dublin alone, while the numerous affairs, liaisons and dalliances which he conducted throughout his life almost certainly produced more.

Oscar Wilde, despite his mother's later extravagant claims for her son's infant abilities, was no child prodigy, nor was his youth obviously pregnant with future greatness. He spent his childhood with his parents in their house at Merrion Square, where he was indulged, but not apparently spoiled by them.

The house was a liberal one. Oscar and his brother were accustomed from a young age to dine with their mother and father, even when they entertained guests, and his brother Willie's later dipsomania has been traced to their early acquaintance with the fruits of the vine.

At the age of ten Oscar was sent with his brother to the staunchly Protestant Portora Royal School, established by Charles II – a curious choice by his mother, who remained a fierce nationalist all her days. Though keenly avoiding organised games and all the other physical activities to which young boys are subjected in vain attempts to subdue their energies, Wilde seems to have liked the school.

Although when his contemporaries tried in later years to recall him there, they could not remember a great deal about the tall, ungainly boy, still, he marked himself out by certain oddities of taste and eccentricities of deportment. A devoted attachment to his silk hat, a stovepipe of immense height, which in contravention of the rules he rarely removed, was one; as was his fondness for the de luxe edition of Æschylus which his schoolmates believed he carried with him everywhere. In early evidence, too, was an aptitude for the *bon mot*: the trenchant nicknames that he devised earned him his comrades' respect and awe, while their tolerance was secured by the wildly exaggerated fantasies that he embroidered out of perfectly mundane experiences for their amusement.

Oscar's time at Portora, though largely uneventful in itself, was punctuated by two experiences in his family, the memory of which were long to remain with him. The death in 1866 of his sister Isola affected him deeply, and led him twenty years later to write *In Memoriam*, one of the most poignant of his sonnets. Less tragically, but more dramatically, in 1864 Speranza appeared for the second time before a Dublin court as the result of her literary efforts; however, this time, the charge was malicious, rather than seditious libel.

Sir William Wilde received a knighthood for his services to the state in 1864. Shortly after, a girl named Mary Travers, with whom the doctor had lately broken off a dalliance of some long standing, began circulating allegations of abduction and rape against him. To be sure of her aim, for good measure she bombarded the house in Merrion Square with copies of her pamphlet, in which Sir William was thinly disguised as the lecherous Dr Quilp.

'Speranza' always knew of and accepted her husband's many infidelities, to the extent that, as Sir William lay dying in 1876, she allowed a woman draped in the black crepe of deepest mourning, whose identity no one knew, to come and sit by him every day, merely because it gave him comfort. Lady Wilde, on the other hand, would not stand by and watch her family's name dragged though the mud. Without informing her husband, she wrote a fierce and deliberately offensive letter to the

Oscar Wilde's birthplace at Westland Row, Dublin. 'Creation begins on the day you were born, and will end on the day you die.'

girl's father, in which she made allegations amounting to prostitution and blackmail against his daughter. Mary discovered the letter, and took out a suit for libel against its author.

At the trial, while the jury found for Travers, their award of a farthing in damages showed that they had no great respect for either party, and their verdict did little to damage the standing of the Wildes in society: despite the questionable wholesomeness of his personal habits and appearance, Sir William's good works and munificent devotion to his poorer patients lent an air of respectability to his personality that seemed to contradict the worst people had heard of him.

The Berkeley Gold Medal for Greek, which Oscar won in 1874. In times of hardship, it was always the last thing to be pawned, and the first to be redeemed.

After six years at Portora during which Oscar had done as little as he could get away with, a late spurt of hard work won him a scholarship to Trinity College, Dublin in 1871. His time at the boarding school had revealed in him a talent for the classics, and he was highly favoured by Fortune in her choice of his tutor. The influence of the Reverend John Mahaffy, the Professor of Ancient History at Trinity, was to do much to transform a sensitive, solitudinous boy into a gregarious, confident young man.

From Mahaffy, a profoundly able scholar in whom all academic, athletic and social graces were united, Wilde learned the lasting lesson of the value of playing to an audience. Mahaffy's affable Dublin snobbery valued social success over most other virtues, and his pupil set about shaping himself according to the master's model. Oscar took up fishing and riding – though he never hunted – canoeing and rowing, and, more importantly, began to sharpen his talent for storytelling. At his parents' house in Merrion Square he found an always appreciative audience, and a mother who was prepared to lead the applause.

Oscar's father, William Wilde, was a noted Dublin doctor knighted for his services to the state. This plaque is on the family home in Merrion Square.

Speranza's youthful activism had made her name in both literary and social Dublin, and to the salon of this female Quixote, whose appearance was never less than striking, some of the the best, as well as some of the oddest, specimens of Dublin society made the weekly journey. As she grew older, so, to comfort her vanity, the house grew darker, and in the gloaming she presided over one of the most distinguished social circles in the country. The easy generosity that Oscar inherited ensured that her 'At Homes' were well attended, and although he lodged at Trinity, he often dined with his parents, by turns amazing and amusing the distinguished assemblies with his ever-increasing wit and charm.

*Oscar Wilde at Magdalen College, Oxford, signally
failing to live up to his blue china. Neither Greek,
gracious, nor, for that matter, uneducated.*

Lady Wilde had but little care for the good opinions of her peers. Bringing a Trinity colleague to Merrion Square one day, Oscar told the friend, 'I want to introduce you to my mother. We have founded a society for the Suppression of Virtue.' Her house was run with the erratic nonchalance of a true bohemian, 'dirty and daring, disorderly and picturesque'. Speranza, scourge of the English, considered herself a member of an aristocracy of letters, believing that as an artist, both she and her family were above the conventional, pious morality of their milieu. Sir William, too, was famous for his slovenliness: Oscar learned arrogance at his parents' knees.

Inspired by Mahaffy's genial tutelage, Wilde did slightly more work than was strictly required of him at Trinity, and his application earned him the Berkeley Gold Medal for Greek composition, and a scholarship to Oxford University worth £95 per annum, which was then a more than substantial sum of money. The medal was to be a double treasure: *in extremis* it was always the first thing to be pawned, and always the first to be redeemed.

There was nothing in the least unmanly about the Oscar Wilde who arrived at Magdalen College, Oxford, in the autumn of 1874. One of the few photographs that survive from this period shows him aged about twenty-one. His Derby hat, the brim barely covering his ears, jammed firmly on one side of his enormous head, and his loud tweed suit show at least that he did not begin his Oxford career as an æsthete. On the contrary, he looked every inch a fashionable, modern, varsity man.

After the religious mania of the Oxford Movement that had swept through it in the previous decades, in the 1870s the university had moved on, and was now in the grip of an æsthetic phase. Magdalen, with its cloisters, its beautiful deer park and its picturesquely medieval atmosphere, was arguably the most æsthetic of Oxford's colleges. The figures of two highly different dons, John Ruskin and Walter Pater, were radical and iconic for artistic young men, and Wilde was soon caught up in their spell.

Ruskin remains one of the most important and original critics of the Victorian era. At the time of Oscar's arrival, his reputation and his mental powers were at their height. In his youth the champion of landscape artist J.M. Turner, Ruskin's middle years were spent rediscovering forgotten aspects of the Italian Renaissance. His was a quintessentially prim, Victorian view of the world. His obsession with the beauty and honesty

Walter Pater was so ugly that his friends begged him to grow this moustache. No one, not even Goethe, was known to pass a butcher's window with as much speed.

On 17 October 1874 Wilde matriculated at
Magdalen College Oxford , being given rooms
No 1, 2 Pair Right in Chaplain's.

of gothic architecture found expression in his masterpiece, *The Stones of Venice*. Similarly, his conception of the Renaissance was based on an ideal of essentially pious artists demonstrating their love for God in their work: the painters and architects of fourteenth-century Florence or sixteenth-century Venice he imagined inspired by a sort of 'muscular Christianity', the fruits of their labour proof of their faith. Hardly interested in the more wordly and pagan aspects of Renaissance art, or the frank sensuality of Michelangelo, his preference was for the pastel ætheriality of the early fresco painters and the curious mysticism of Tintoretto.

Cushioned by considerable personal wealth, Ruskin was able to develop the theory – greatly reinforced by his personal contact with the Pre-Raphælite movement and later echoed in the ideals of William Morris – that art was a vital and essential part of life, not merely an adjunct to existence only to be enjoyed by an educated few. Gradually the idea began to gain a wider currency, but his attempts to put such ideals into practice demonstrate both the considerable strengths and the abundant weaknesses of such æsthetic theories.

The Acropolis in Greece, 'not ruins, but ruins of
those ruins', visited by Oscar with J.P. Mahaffy on
their Grand Tour of 1877.

The so-called Hinksey Road Campaign involved the building of a lane to connect two Oxfordshire villages separated by swamp; the project was devised by Ruskin to give his students a practical insight into the dignity of labour and the supposed satisfaction that even the most educated might obtain from hard physical work. Unfortunately the road was, at least materially, an abject failure: both Ruskin and his students, Oscar among them, were incompetent at the work, and the road was abandoned after a year, barely half-finished. Ruskin eventually imported his own gardener to rescue the enterprise from total ignominy. The chief attraction the project held for the undergraduates was rather less the purifying nature of the work than the lavish breakfast that invariably followed, where they were able to talk informally with the master.

That Wilde was at first heavily influenced by Ruskin was evident in the decoration of his rooms, which were hung with photographic reproductions of the kind of pictures – mostly Renaissance figure subjects – the professor thought most improving. But Ruskin's magnetic personality was removed when he went to Venice at the end of 1876, and the mantle of æsthetic mentor passed on to Walter Pater. Although he had once been one of Ruskin's enthusiastic followers, Pater was now preaching a very much more advanced æsthetic creed.

Wilde might have been thinking of Ruskin when he wrote of a particular critic that he 'had succeeded in raising painting to the status of manual labour'. He could not have been referring to Walter Pater. The hothouse atmosphere of Pater's *Studies in the History of the Renaissance*, published in 1873, wherein he stressed the overriding importance of sensation, and denied that art should have any concern with morality, was in total contrast to the current of even unconventional thought at Oxford. It was also far more alluringly dangerous.

Pater rejected utterly the Victorian ideal of the marriage between art and morality. In the 'Conclusion' to his *Studies in the History of the Renaissance* – later suppressed for fear it would 'lead young men astray' – he more fully expounded his theory that art was the end in itself. Art had no business preaching morals when it should be proclaiming only beauty: 'our one chance lies in getting as many pulsations into the given time,' he wrote. Pater advocated 'the love of art for art's sake'; for 'Art comes to you proposing frankly to give nothing but the highest quality to your moments as they pass.' Pater preached, above all, intensity: 'To burn always with this hard gemlike flame is success in life.'

Pater was undoubtedly homosexually inclined, and drew about him only the prettiest of the undergraduates. His private sexual tendencies were repressed, however, and this self-imposed constraint made him morbidly shy and socially inept. Having attended a lecture which Pater closed with 'I hope you all heard me,' Wilde was reported to have muttered, 'We overheard you'. Despite provoking such good-humoured ragging, Pater had a lasting intellectual and æsthetic influence on Wilde's generation at Oxford, and his ideals pervaded every aspect of their lives. Oscar's rooms, which were supposed to have been the 'best' at Magdalen, rapidly came to reflect his new master's philosophy. They became more and more curiously bedecked with exclusive *objets d'art*, exquisite Japanese fans and a very fine collection of blue-and-white china.

With rarefied tastes came a more refined persona, and 1877 found Wilde conscientiously experimenting with artificial poses and positions. His talk, from being merely witty or clever, began to assume something of that oracular obscurity that he was later fully to incorporate into his personality. One night, wistfully surveying his rooms, he was heard to sigh, 'I find it harder every day to live up to my blue china'. Both his friends and his enemies were delighted with the remark. It was bandied about Oxford until it reached the ear of a fearsomely bewhiskered university dean, who, outraged, in a sermon at St Mary's, declared war on this 'form of heathenism, which it is our bounden duty to fight against'. The skirmish was Oscar's first real taste of fame and notoriety: he liked it, and did everything in his power to attract and cultivate it henceforth.

In Kipling's poem 'The Mary Gloster', a dying captain of the Empire berates his artistic son with the following lines:

'The things I knew was proper, you wouldn't thank me to give,
And the things I knew was rotten, you said was the way to live.
For you muddled with books an' pictures, an' china an' etchings and fans,
And your rooms at college was beastly, more like a whore's than a man's.'

It could have been against Wilde's circle that the poem was directed.

Though members of his circle were notably affectionate with each other, Wilde did not share all of Pater's tastes, for at a certain point he contracted syphilis from a local girl, and during the usual – and of course totally ineffective – course of mercury treatments, his teeth turned black.

Clever young men of the nineteenth century were almost honour-bound to write poetry, and the mainspring of Wilde's poetical inspiration at Oxford was the Church of Rome. Like many of his friends, he was attracted to the magnificence, the solemnity and the ritual of the Catholic Church, but he did not convert, owing to the consequent threat of disinheritance that hung over him. This spectre was removed in 1876 with the death of his father.

In the early spring of 1877, Wilde joined a party, assembled by his old Dublin tutor Mahaffy, on its way to Greece. The trip seemingly put the final seal on his religious 'wobbles'. When the party stopped in Rome, his friend David Hunter Blair, himself shortly to become a priest, arranged an audience with the Pope. Wilde was deeply impressed, and with his rapidly increasing understanding of the importance of theatrical gesture, kissed the Papal Ring with enthusiasm. But the party continued on to Greece with nothing finally consummated, and at Athens, Oscar's unfeigned love of the classics was confirmed. He was able to see clearly that Rome had no monopoly on the intelligent patronage of art and, although the Christian religions continued in an abstract way to fascinate him, and the figure of Christ was to come to obsess him, there

Newdigate Prize Poem.

RAVENNA.

RECITED IN

THE THEATRE, OXFORD,

JUNE 26, 1878.

BY

OSCAR WILDE,
MAGDALEN COLLEGE.

with the author's compliments

OXFORD:
THOS. SHRIMPTON AND SON, BROAD-STREET.
1878.

The title-page of Ravenna, *the poem Oscar wrote for the Newdigate Prize of 1878. He was inspired by the mediæval town in which the exiled poet Dante died.*

was no more serious talk of conversion until immediately before his death. For a while at least, his talk was instead all of Greek ideals.

Mahaffy's group spent longer away than they had initially intended, and Wilde did not return to Oxford until well after the beginning of the spring term. Fined by the proctors, and with his scholarship monies retained, it looked for a time as though he would be forced to go down from the university in disgrace. However, on the announcement of the theme set for the Newdigate Prize, the annual poetry competition won in the past by Ruskin and Matthew Arnold, he must have laughed for joy: the subject set for 1878 was Ravenna, a city that he had visited only nine months before. It need hardly be added that he won, or that his declamation of the poem met with a rapturous reception.

Oscar left Oxford with the expected double first, and the most prestigious prize available to an undergraduate. His poems were beginning to receive attention in newspapers and journals. He knew, and was known by, London society: Wilde's future was looking rosy.

The outstanding student of his year, for some time after leaving Oxford he entertained the idea that his abilities might, like Pater's, languidly adorn the

A late photograph of the painter Frank Miles. Oscar's parting words to him were 'I will leave you. I will go now, and I will never speak to you again as long as I live.'

groves of academe. He attempted to obtain Oxford fellowships in classics and archæology, but a shortage of posts, combined with a reluctance on the part of the university authorities to trust a man who had been so controversial and flamboyant as an undergraduate, conspired to dash his hopes. This was, in truth, fortunate: his utter unsuitability for tasks requiring sustained effort would have made him miserable, and he would have, as he wrote of 'poor dear Pater', 'lived to disprove everything he has written'.

It was in the pose of 'art critic and professor of æsthetics' that Wilde took up residence in London at the beginning of 1879. During his time at Oxford, frequent visits to London had won him the acquaintance of several duchesses and other leaders of society, as well as such fashionable theatrical

The famous beauty Lillie Langtry, who charmed Edward, Prince of Wales, and conquered London High Society with nothing but her beauty and a single black dress.

figures as Ellen Terry, Henry Irving and the brilliant and waspish painter James McNeill Whistler, known to his friends and many enemies as Jimmy.

Initially, at least, Oscar's entrée into high society came largely through another painter, his friend Frank Miles, a Royal Academician. They had been introduced by Miles's friend – and probable lover – Lord Ronald Gower, with whom Oscar was at Oxford; many of the pictures that had supplanted the Botticelli photographs in Wilde's rooms had been by Miles. Gower's sister was the Duchess of Westminster, and, through her patronage, the artist's star rose until he became one of the most fashionable portraitists of his day. Winner of the Turner Prize in 1880, nevertheless Frank Miles laboured under a terrible disability as an artist: being almost totally colour-blind, he was only really capable of work in pencil and charcoal, although Ruskin had praised him in those strange words that ring down the ages: 'with his love for his mother and his ability to paint clouds he must get on'.

Wilde and Miles took rooms in a house at 13 Salisbury Street. 'Untidy and romantic,' it was facetiously renamed Thames House for its (nonexistent) views of the river. The two men set about decorating their set in a high æsthetic style, and soon the most prominent ladies of society could be seen at Salisbury Street. Their lifestyle became increasingly extravagant and expensive. On his death, Sir William Wilde had left to his younger son a little money and some houses in Dublin, on the income from which Oscar had, without conspicuous success, attempted to live while he was at Oxford. A desperate need for more unfettered access to the capital the properties represented led him to sell them in 1878. The £2,800 he realized from the sale was equivalent perhaps to more than half a million pounds today, but the money did not last very long. Before it went, however, it fully instilled in him an open-handed financial generosity, which was, in the end, to exacerbate the difficulties that led to his fall. For the moment, though, his pockets were filled with gold, and Oscar set out to carve himself a place in society. He secured invitations to every fashionable gathering, and conquered both his hostesses and their friends with his dazzling displays of wit, charm and brazen insolence.

Miles's vogue brought to his studio some of the great beauties of London, both as patrons and as friends, and while there they were entertained by Oscar's increasingly entrancing conversation. Miles and he also developed a passion for the stage, in particular the Lyceum, which the great actor-manager Henry Irving's tenure had made into a prime social gathering place, and they adored the company of actresses, whose gaiety and freedom from convention amused them, and whose late hours meant that they were perfect company.

Perhaps the most beautiful of the menagerie of these so-called 'Professional Beauties' who visited Thames House was Lillie Langtry, the closest thing to a home-grown *demi-mondaine* in the Parisian mode that the English could boast since the retirement of 'Skittles' Walters. Lillie's voluptuousness was in marked contrast to the languorous appearance of the Pre-Raphælite *belles*, and when she arrived from Jersey in 1876 with nothing but a 'fat and uninteresting husband', her beauty and a single black evening gown, she had immediately been accorded by all society the status of a minor goddess.

G.F. Watts, Frederic Leighton and Whistler begged her to sit for them, to which she agreed with the alacrity of one who has nothing to lose and much to gain. Millais's painting of her with a lily – only many years later did an amateur botanist notice that the one she was holding was from Guernsey – earned her the sobriquet of the Jersey Lily. When Wilde met her, soon after her debut, through Miles, he called her 'the loveliest woman in Europe'. Her description of him was less flattering: 'He had a well-shaped mouth, with somewhat coarse lips and greenish-hued teeth. The plainness of his face, however, was redeemed by the splendour of his great, eager eyes.' He superintended her wardrobe, and pouted when she did not follow his sartorial advice. Rapidly becoming obsessed, Wilde used, according to popular but doubtless apocryphal legend, to sleep outside her St James's house every night, and bring her a fresh lily every morning.

Lillie grew tired of the poet's constant attention, and became romantically involved with the Prince of Wales, who would refuse to go to parties unless his mistress was also invited. Lillie extended a similar largesse to Wilde, and persuaded the Prince publicly to request a meeting with her

Ellen Terry: 'She stands with eyes marred by the mists of pain,/Like some wan lily overdrenched with rain.'

friend. With generous humour, he accordingly pronounced at a party a short time later, 'I do not know Mr Wilde, and not to know Mr Wilde is not to be known.' The following week, the corpulent but stately figure of the future king was seen ascending the stairs at Thames House.

Wilde and Miles were only two among the legion of admirers who flocked about Ellen Terry, Irving's leading lady at the Lyceum, but in the sonnet Wilde wrote in praise of her in the role of Queen Henrietta Maria she recognized a particular sincerity and talent:

> *'She stands with eyes marred with the mists of pain,*
> *Like some wan lily overdrenched with rain.'*

They also knew Sarah Bernhardt, the great French actress equally at home playing either Ophelia or Hamlet, and Wilde's increasing notoriety helped to promote her fame when she arrived in England in 1879. As she disembarked at Folkestone docks she was met with the cry of '*Vive* Sarah Bernhardt,' and Oscar, in what was becoming his usual manner of paying tribute, cast a bunch of lilies at her feet.

Attracted by the lilies and his highly theatrical costume, the attention of the press, and in particular *Punch*'s cartoonist George du Maurier began to be trained on Wilde. Du Maurier, who dubbed him variously Drawit Milde, Oscuro Wildegoose and Ossian Wilderness, represented him as the apotheosis of æstheticism, all flowing locks and lilies.

Wilde's relations with painters were always ambiguous: although he knew as much about art as many professional critics, his own view, which grew in conviction over the years, was that painting was a relatively inferior practice, and that the greatest of the arts, because the most suggestive, was poetry. He found most painters dull and literal-minded, and in their turn, the sober Academicians were never fond of Wilde. W.P. Frith's 'Private View at the Royal Academy' of 1881 included what was intended to be a hostile representation of the poet, who stands in the very centre of the fashionable Royal Academy crowd. Frith's idea was to mock the high-priest of æstheticism, but, surrounded by adoring young women, Wilde's prominence in the picture and the clearly magnetic personality that shines through Frith's disdain make him its star.

The one artist for whom at this time he had an unqualified admiration was Jimmy Whistler, the dandified American whose paintings, though highly controversial, were radically modern and utterly original. Charles Ricketts used to describe him, 'with his yellow tie, wasp-waist, beige-coloured overcoat, wand-like stick and flat-brimmed top hat', as resembling nothing more than 'a Hungarian band-master'. One of the great artists of the century, he was also one of the most splendidly arrogant and vexatious of

RIGHT: *'St Oscar of Oxford, poet and martyr' among friends in the University City he called the most beautiful thing in England.*

men. He won the libel suit he pressed against Ruskin after the critic had declared of one painting that he 'never expected to hear a coxcomb ask two hundred guineas for flinging a pot of paint in the public's face'; awarded the traditional farthing's damages, Whistler was bankrupted by the costs. Wilde provided the vain, quick-tempered painter with an appreciative audience, and Jimmy in his turn taught Wilde much about how, by boldness and bravado, hostility could be countered and turned to advantage.

The 'Apostle of Æstheticism' was also, by now, a poet of considerable power. Having written poems since his boyhood, Oscar took his art seriously enough to physically assault a Trinity man who had dared to mock one of his compositions. It was at Trinity that Wilde's poems were initially published – the first, 'From Spring Days to Winter', appeared in the Dublin University Magazine in 1876, followed by others both there and, probably through the influence of his mother, in the *Irish Monthly*.

In between dinner engagements and his vain pursuit of Lillie Langtry, Wilde spent increasing amounts of time writing his delicate verses. In 1880 he started to search for a publisher. Having hawked his manuscripts around several, Wilde was forced into private publication by their refusal to take him seriously. At that date this route was by no means reserved only for poetasters, and the book, entitled simply *Poems*, was, from the point of view of sales, a great success, going through four editions in as many weeks. The critics were not as enthusiastic as the public. Even the most generous notice said that the work was impossible to review, being neither good nor bad, but merely indifferent.

The copy that was requested by the Oxford Union Debating Society met with a uniquely harsh fate: a vote of thanks for the gift was proposed, but the volume's acceptance was objected to by an undergraduate. He said that the verses it contained were 'for the most part not by their putative father at all, but by a number of better-known and more deservedly reputed authors. The Union Library already contains better and fuller editions of all these poets: and I move that it be not accepted.' To the embarrassment of the committee, *Poems* was returned to its author.

But Oscar was already discovering that 'there is only one thing worse than being talked about, and that is not being talked about'. He was to learn the truth of his most famous maxim over the next ten years. *Poems* was talked about endlessly, and largely detrimentally, despite the fact that those few who actually read it were disappointed to discover nothing obscene in the vein of 'the fleshly school of poetry', but only a Frenchified amorality which, to advanced readers, was already becoming *passé*.

The publication of *Poems* had an unforeseen effect: the loss of a friendship. Frank Miles's father, a canon in the Church, objected to his son's relationship with the notorious Mr Wilde, and demanded that he cut so scandalous a friend. Miles, financially dependent on his father, was obliged to obey, and Wilde left the house they had moved into in Tite Street, Chelsea – and upon which he had spent much of his small fortune in decorating – deeply hurt. His generous nature would have taken no delight in the rapid falling away of patronage that led to Miles's untimely death in a lunatic asylum a few years later.

A portrait of Sarah Bernhardt. Oscar said of her voice that it made water as exhilarating as wine. When he was down on his luck she refused to help him.

PATIENCE

D'OYLY CARTE OPERA COMPANY

CHAPTER TWO

Declaring His Genius

P ATIENCE, A GENTLE *enough Gilbert and Sullivan operetta satirizing æstheticism and the æsthetes, opened at the London Opera Comique in 1881. Its two main characters are composites of Algernon Swinburne, Wilde, Whistler and Frank Miles, but the timeliness of the skit, coinciding, in the wake of* Poems, *with Wilde's first period of fame, ensured that Wilde's name was the one most closely associated with the work. It was a considerable popular hit, and transferred to D'Oyly Carte's Savoy Theatre during the summer, where it ran to packed houses every night.*

Wilde appears to have shared in the amusement of the *Punch*-reading public at *Patience*, for although elements in the character of Bunthorne, who 'walked up Piccadilly with a lily in his medieval

ABOVE: *Wilde arrived in New York on the SS* Arizona. *'I am not exactly pleased with the Atlantic Ocean. It is not so majestic as I had expected.'*

LEFT: *Gilbert and Sullivan's Bunthorne, the first of many caricatures of Oscar Wilde: the kind of homage that mediocrity always pays to genius.*

hand', were specifically directed against him, it was by no means a direct caricature, and his friendship with the actor playing Bunthorne ensured that at least some punches were pulled.

D'Oyly Carte produced *Patience* on Broadway during the autumn of the same year, where it enjoyed such full houses that the impresario saw the possibility of broadening its renown – and filling his own pockets – by exporting Wilde to a market anxious to get a closer view of the original of one of these fey æsthetic creatures. In October 1881, D'Oyly Carte's New York offices telegraphed to Wilde, proposing that, subject to the success of a trial period, he embark on a lecture tour of the United States comprising fifty engagements, with guaranteed fees and all expenses paid.

Brooklyn Bridge, New York, by R. Schwartz. The newly built bridge would have greeted Wilde, the man André Gide called 'the most dangerous product of modern civilisation', as he arrived to claim the New World.

Max Beerbohm capturing in caricature the moment
in 1882 when the name of Dante Gabriel Rossetti
was first heard in America.

A prouder, duller man would have treated the offer as an insulting practical joke, but whilst his acceptance is evidence of his desire for publicity and his habitual good humour at jokes made at his own expense, his consideration of such a proposal reveals, even more, his chronic want of money. 'Yes, if offer good,' was his reply. It was plainly good enough, for three months later, on Christmas Eve, he embarked from Liverpool on his way to introduce his creed to the New World.

He took with him an extraordinary set of costumes that he had had specially made. Some of these, including a 'befrogged and wonderfully befurred green overcoat', he had tried out on his friends before he left. Whistler did not approve: 'How dare you!' he shrieked at Oscar in a letter to *The World*, 'What means this unseemly carnival in my Chelsea! Restore these things to Nathan, and never let me find you masquerading in the combined costumes of a degraded Kossuth and Mr Mantalini.'

Oscar in æsthetic mode in 1882. He would later
remark of his American costume, 'Strange that a
pair of silk stockings should so upset a nation.'

The crowd of journalists that awaited Wilde's arrival at the New York dockside was somewhat confused by the curiously attired giant who stepped off the SS *Arizona*: *Patience* had characterized the æsthetes as wan and decadent creatures who practically ate flowers, and the gentleman in the fur-trimmed, bottle-green greatcoat did not quite conform to expectations. Like children presented with a long-awaited toy, the journalists were abashed in his presence, and Oscar answered their stupid questions in a bored and offhand manner. He moved on to the Custom House, where every expectation of his precocity was finally fulfilled. 'I have nothing to declare,' he told the customs officers, and after a dramatic pause worthy of Irving himself, and which he had undoubtedly been practising since he left London, he added, 'except my genius'.

Questioning of his fellow passengers proved a more fertile source of Wilde's epigrammatic wit, though perhaps not an accurate one. One of the passengers recalled the following: 'I am not exactly pleased with the Atlantic Ocean. It is not so majestic as I had expected.' The journalists had their headlines; Wilde's fame was doubly secured.

Throughout his American tour Oscar's every move was dogged by the press, who, invariably hostile, either could not or would not leave him alone. This was to be a recurrent feature of his life: the American journalists thought him a poor joke, and when he treated them like a poorer one, they were driven into frenzies of jealousy and hate by the self-appointed prophet of the æsthetic movement. Their hostility was self-defeating, however, for it aroused the curiosity of the public, who flocked to the lecture halls in ever greater numbers to see for themselves this strange new flower of English decadence.

Oscar Wilde was welcomed with open arms by New York society. Staying at the Grand Hotel on Broadway, he received far more invitations than he could sensibly cope with. Being a profoundly social creature, he accepted as many engagements as he was able, until quite worn out by the exertion. He did, however, think it prudent to tone down his usual insolence for his American hostesses.

The Chickering Hall in New York was packed to the rafters with eager listeners for Wilde's first lecture on 9 January 1882. In a 'dark purple sack coat and knee-breeches; black hose, low shoes with black buckles; a frill of rich lace at the wrists; hair long, and parted in the middle' he took his notes from a morocco case, and lectured gravely for an hour. 'Strange,' he later wrote, 'that a pair of silk stockings should so upset a nation.'

Colonel W.F. Morse, who organised the tour on Carte's behalf, had but a poor grasp of American geography, and Wilde set off on an eccentric odyssey across the country. Wilde relied largely on a single lecture on interior decoration entitled 'The House Beautiful', which he declaimed in town after town to

A THING OF BEAUTY NOT A JOY FOREVER.
Rise and Fall of a "Vera" Wilde Æsthete.

*'A thing of beauty not a joy for ever.' The view of an American
satirist, published in 1883, who enjoyed misquoting Keats almost
as much as Wilde did himself. Although he made many friends
once the novelty wore off the bricks began to fly*

the delight of the townswomen, and the scorn of its men. Even their scorn generally lasted only as long as Oscar Wilde was merely a name to his hearers. After the shock of his appearance wore off and he began to talk, his easy charm and civility hushed the most hostile crowd.

One night at Boston, a detachment of swells from Harvard University decided to put Wilde on the spot. Sixty of them engaged the front rows of the auditorium and with the utmost solemnity trooped in wearing velvet breeches and carrying lilies. To their dismay Oscar had received word of the prank, and appeared in evening clothes of perfect convention. Having been mobbed by hearties at Oxford, he was not without experience in asserting his authority, and good-humouredly twitted, ragged and teased the embarrassed boys throughout the talk. Observing that he 'seemed to see certain signs of an artistic movement in the lecture hall', he wove effortlessly into the fabric of his talk covert insults such as 'caricature is the tribute mediocrity pays to genius', and closed with the prayer, 'Save me from my disciples'. When the students of Yale attempted to repeat the jest it fell even flatter.

During the tour Oscar introduced himself to most of the lions of American literature. In Boston he met a then almost unknown writer called Henry James, who, although he was initially impressed by the young man, soon tired of his flippancy, never suspecting that it might in fact have been a serious disguise. James was later to include a hostile caricature of Wilde in his novel *The Tragic Muse*. By chance the then elderly niece of the poet Keats was present at one of Wilde's lectures, and she was so impressed by what she saw and heard that she presented him with the original manuscript of Keats's 'Sonnet on Blue', which he was always to treasure. And in Connecticut Oscar sought an audience with that venerable old paederast Walt Whitman. He succeeded in making such a conquest of America's foremost poet that he ever after claimed still to feel Whitman's parting kiss on his lips.

Several months of touring the eastern seaboard and Canada were followed by a trek to the wilds of California, where he thought it prudent to subdue the more outlandish of his sartorial effects, but even the rough westerners fell under his spell. Wilde, in his turn, was impressed by their rugged honesty and pragmatic attitude to art. A sign in a bar entreating patrons: 'Please don't shoot the pianist, he is doing his best,' Oscar praised as 'the only rational method of art criticism I have ever come across'.

Nevertheless, one suspects that the western miners to whom he lectured on the Renaissance were less impressed by Oscar's taste, than his ability, at dinners consisting of 'first course, whiskey, the second, whiskey, the third, whiskey', to drink them under the table. 'I spoke to them of the early Florentines, and they slept as though no crime had ever stained the ravines of their mountain home,' he said. He described Whistler's painting, and 'in their grand simple style' they were outraged: 'such things should not be, they cried. Some of the younger ones pulled out their revolvers and left to see if Jimmy was "prowling about the saloons"'.

Mary Anderson, Wilde's first and last Duchess of Padua. He contemplated writing a tragedy, entitled 'Death of the Duchess,' about her performance.

Wilde's early friend and subsequent enemy James Abbot McNeill Whistler, 'a miniature Mephistopheles, mocking the majority,' in the bravura painting by Boldini.

Wilde remained in America for several months after the lecture tour ended, enjoying his popularity and trying to arrange for a production, by the actress Marie Prescott, of his first play, *Vera, or the Nihilists*. He had also aroused the interest of Mary Anderson, another potential actress/patroness, in his second – as yet unwritten – play, *The Duchess of Padua*. By the end of the year, though, it became clear that *Vera* would not immediately be produced, and he returned to England.

Having spent January 1883 uneventfully in London, hoping to conquer Paris as he had captured London, New York and Boston, in February Oscar set out for France, taking with him letters of intro-duction and several presentation copies of his *Poems*. These ambassadors he sent to all the leading French artists and literary figures, and with such cartes-de-visite as his verses he had the entrée to many places barred to a more conventional writer. He visited the great names of the older generation, Edmond de Goncourt, Emile Zola and the dying Victor Hugo, but also met younger lions, including the Symbolist poet Paul Verlaine, and dined with Degas and the Pissarros. He also came across a man who was to become one of his most constant and faithful friends. Robert Sherard, a melancholic exile, loathed Wilde at first sight, but soon came to regard him as part saint, part conquering hero, and was to be his first – if imperfect – hagiographer.

'The great superiority of France over England,' Wilde once said, 'is that in France every bourgeois wants to be an artist, whereas in England every artist wants to be a bourgeois.' He always loved Paris, and later in his life would go there in moments of distress or elation, success or failure, finding a secu-rity in the freemasonry of letters lacking in London.

Wilde's style of dress changed radically during his stay in Paris: the former æsthetic posturing was replaced with a severe dandyism in the mid-century style of Baudelaire. Word of the indecency of his skin-tight trousers earned him a reproach from his mother, now living in London with his brother Willie. Oscar discovered an artistic barber, with whom he went to the Louvre to see busts, and commiserated about the ignorance of the public in the face of a work of art. Shortly thereafter, he had his flowing locks cut and curled in the manner of Nero.

Only the fur-lined overcoat, which he carted about the States – 'to hide the ugliness of the sofas' – he would not discard, and this remaining affectation earned him some hostility amongst Parisian *gens littéraires*, who associated ostentation – at least involving fur – with the bourgeoisie. The French could never understand the point of his American fopperies: Degas's piercing wit gave tongue to the commonly held view that 'he has the look of an amateur playing Lord Byron in a suburban theatre'.

Despite a hectic social life, Wilde still managed to finish the *Duchess of Padua* only a little after Mary Anderson's March deadline. In a letter he described the play as '*the chef d'œuvre* of my youth,' but his opinion was not shared by the actress. Sherard reports that the news of her rejection of his 'master-piece' Wilde received with little outward sign of despair. 'We shall not be dining with the Duchess tonight,' he said; but having been living high in expectation of the $4,000 she had promised, financial pressures forced a return to London. Not, however, before he had given Sherard, with extraordinary generosity, enough money to leave his exile in Paris and join him in London.

Meanwhile in America, Marie Prescott was finally ready to produce *Vera*, and Wilde crossed the Atlantic again in July to be present at rehearsals. The audience at the première, despite the sweltering heat of a New York August, loved the first half, and at the curtain of Act II loudly demanded the 'Author'. The second half was not so well received, and the summons was not repeated. The reviews were dismissive: 'Vera bad,' wrote one wag. On this occasion the critics were not, given the quality of the play or the acting – Wilde himself was forced privately to revise his opinion of Miss Prescott's abilities – greatly unfair, for the work is undoubtedly not its author's finest hour.

In a desperate attempt to stave off closure, attempts were made to persuade Oscar to take over the role of Prince Paul, but he refused to act – on stage at least. The play closed after only a week, and Wilde somewhat dejectedly returned home.

On his return from Paris Wilde had found the quondam manager of his American tour, Colonel Morse, in London, and proposed that their former success could be repeated in England. Morse agreed, and started to organise dates around the country.

In view of the failure of both of his attempts on the stage, a new lecture tour now became a measure more and more essential to stem Wilde's haemorrhaging finances. Having long since run through his patrimony, Oscar had been forced to dip into the earnings from his American tour to support himself in Paris, and now of those, too, there was little left. In anticipation of receipts, he borrowed £1,200 and tried, with no more success than before, to economise. Morse later estimated that

Les Décadents: The Social Life in Paris

1.

2.

3.

4.

5.

6.

1: *Victor Hugo by Leon Bonnat, the only man to sleep through an audience with Oscar Wilde.*

2: *Stephan Mallarmé, the sinless master of obscure verse, by Jaques-Emile Blanche.*

3: *Verlaine and Rimbaud, both seated at left 'talking of purple things, and drinking of purple wine' (by Henri Fantin-Latour).*

4: *André Gide by Jaques-Emile Blanche, whom Oscar 'taught to lie until his lips curled.'*

5: *Wilde at the Folies Bergères: H. de Toulouse Lautrec.*

6: *Count Robert de Montesquiou, the model for Huysman's des Esseintes, by Boldini.*

he had arranged for Wilde more than 150 lectures and with fees of ten or fifteen guineas per appearance, this must have represented a considerable improvement in his client's prospects. Wilde must have known, though, that the burden of his debts would soon overwhelm him, and at the age of twenty-seven his thoughts turned to marriage.

He had contemplated the step several times in the later 1870s. His pursuit of Florence Balcombe had been foiled by the appearance of Bram Stoker, then manager of the Lyceum; to the writer Violet Hunt, who later settled with Ford Madox Ford, he had proposed in 1880; and his offer of marriage to the heiress Charlotte Montefiore was politely turned down. Her refusal met with the following note:

'Charlotte,

'I am so sorry about your decision. With your money and my brains, we could have gone far.'

In November 1883 Wilde wrote to Lillie Langtry – now a fashionable, if never very good, actress – of the news that he had become engaged to Miss Constance Lloyd, 'a grave, slight, violet-eyed little Artemis'. Though she belonged to an eminently respectable family whom the Wildes had known in Dublin, Oscar only met his future wife for the first time at a 'young person's party' at Constance's grandfather's house at Lancaster Gate in 1881. He was instantly attracted by her. Legend relates that, leaving the party, he informed Lady Wilde, 'By the by, Mama, I think of marrying that girl.'

Constance was no great heiress, and the notion that he married her solely for a fortune may be discounted. Her personal jointure was sufficient to maintain no more than a modest style of life, and the expectations she had on the death of her grandfather, John Horace Lloyd, were never such as to make them her chief charm, especially when London was filled with many other girls with much more impressive qualifications in the financial line.

After his return from America, Wilde's interest in Constance was not initially such as to keep him from the pleasures of society. Nevertheless, during the course of 1883, despite an avowedly cynical view of marriage, he grew to be sincerely in love with the serious, gentle girl. Constance was flattered and overwhelmed by the attentions of the famous poet. She always claimed that he was natural, sincere and unaffected in her company, and he respected her enough to solicit her opinion of his work. Her admiration for his plays and for their author was, however, as she told him, always mixed with a disapproval of what she considered to be their immorality. He should have taken note then of the strong strain of Dublin conformism that ran in her veins.

While preparing for his British lecture tour, Wilde was asked to give a talk on art to the students of the Royal Academy, and boasted of the invitation to his friends. Whistler, from whom the same

RIGHT: *Wilde in an uncharacteristically melancholy pose, considering the relative value of 'the lover's crown of myrtle' and 'the poet's crown of bays'.*

honour had never been solicited, enthusiastically discussed ideas and theories with the man he regarded as his disciple, and Oscar used many of the ideas in the lecture. The general tone of the ensuing talk he delivered can be summed up in his own statement that 'all pictures that do not immediately give you such artistic joy as to make you say "How beautiful", are bad pictures'.

After the Academy lecture, Whistler questioned his protégé on what he had said. As Wilde related each new theme, the painter stood and bowed deeply in self-acknowledgement. These suggestions of plagiarism were made even more pointed in their famous exchange at a private view. Whistler was, as usual, instructing a critic in his business: 'My dear fellow, you must never say this painting is good or bad, but you may say, "I like this," or, "I don't like that." Now come and have a whisky: you're sure to like that.' Wilde, standing by, voiced his admiration, laughing, 'I wish I had said that!' 'You will, Oscar, you will,' replied the painter, with a dry, mirthless chuckle.

The two men had been engaged in energetic and largely good-natured public *badinage* for some time, but tension between the two most æsthetic dandies in London was beginning to attract notice in the press. When *Punch* published in 1883 an imaginary conversation between the two on the state of the theatre, Whistler arranged for the telegrams which passed between them in response to the piece to be published. Oscar's, '*Punch* too ridiculous. When you and I are together we never talk about anything except ourselves,' was met by Whistler's, 'No, no, Oscar, you forget. We never talk about anything but me.' Unfairly, he omitted Oscar's last word: 'It is true, Jimmy, we were talking about you; but I was thinking about myself.'

The snub Whistler assumed the Royal Academy had offered him was not forgotten, and he set about organising a lecture of his own. He arranged, to increase the éclat, what came to be known as 'Mr. Whistler's Ten O'Clock' at that unheard-of hour in the evening, and in the course of his talk, which was attended by all the fashionable critics and socialites, the painter poured out his scorn for the 'dilletante.' All knew this to refer to Wilde. 'The voice of the æsthete,' Whistler lamented, 'is heard in the land, and catastrophe is upon us.'

Oscar displayed humour and tact in the face of Whistler's brazen assault, but the painter had by now lost his sense of humour. Their fight came to a final head in 1890 in the pages of the magazine *Truth*, to which Whistler wrote with a swingeing personal attack on his former friend. 'It is a trouble,' replied Wilde in the same pages, 'for any gentleman to have to notice the lucubrations of so ill-bred and ignorant a person as Mr Whistler.' Delighted that he had finally managed to sting the the poet, Whistler's reply accused Wilde of not being a gentleman at all. Fifty years earlier, a like exchange

LEFT: *Constance Wilde and the couple's first son Cyril. Wilde described her as 'a grave, slight, violet-eyed little Artemis, with great coils of heavy brown hair, which make her flower-like head droop like a blossom.'*

between London's foremost dandies would have resulted in pistols at dawn, but realising that there was no sense, and some danger, in continuing to expose himself to the unpredictable painter's ire, Wilde terminated their contact, public and private, and Whistler was left to snipe from the wings.

٭ ٭ ٭

Wilde's lecture tour of England commenced in September 1883. Colonel Morse's understanding of British geography proved to be no firmer than it had been of American, and his client spent the next six months criss-crossing the country between engagements, one day in Glasgow, the next in London, the next in Newcastle. What joy Oscar could take in insulting the decorations of his provincial patrons was tempered by the financial pressures that formed the mainspring of his inspiration, and his performances often lacked the lustre and exuberance that he had displayed in America.

The tour featured a modified version of the old 'House Beautiful' lecture, and for the sake of variety Wilde added a new talk, 'Personal Reminiscences of America'. The latter, for which his rough *aides-mémoire* survive, was better received than the former, for it gave him a free rein to exercise his ever-sharpening wit without alienating his audiences. If they were led to expect a cross between a lion and a peacock, the polite and soberly dressed young man who lectured to them with all solemnity on the deficiencies in their taste did not always please: many demanded their money back. Having stated in America that 'to disagree with three-fourths of the British public is one of the deepest consolations in moments of spiritual doubt', Wilde did not overly concern himself about their dissatisfaction, and usually made a fast enough exit from the venues not to be obliged to notice it.

November saw Oscar lecturing in Ireland, and there, too, was Constance Lloyd. She attended all his lectures, and he took her about the Dublin theatres; he visited her at home, and she made her pleasure at his attentions plain. Although not without first-hand experience in the subtle art of proposing marriage, Wilde seemed hesitant to cross the Rubicon with Constance, sensing perhaps that he had found someone likely to accept his advances. Nevertheless after some very pointed hints, by which her family made it clear that they viewed Oscar as her suitor, he was persuaded to ask Constance for her hand.

There was little chance that he would this time be rebuffed. 'Prepare yourself for an astounding piece of news!' she wrote to her brother, Otho. 'I am engaged to Oscar Wilde and perfectly and insanely happy.'

John Lloyd had been surprisingly well disposed toward his granddaughter's æsthete suitor, who had recently been castigated in the press as 'unmanly', 'epicene' and a 'Mary-Ann', all journalistic code-words for homosexuals. His only objection was, on the grounds of Wilde's debts, to an early wedding, insisting that Wilde demonstrate his capacity to earn an income. To that end Oscar proposed to write the old man a sonnet on the spot, but was more prosaically required to produce his accounts.

W.P. Frith's painting of a Private View at the Royal Academy *in 1881. In these early years Wilde was constantly surrounded by adoring female admirers, a wrapt audience who hung on his every opinion and 'scandalous' remarks.*

On the morning of their wedding in late May, 1884, Whistler, amiable for the moment, telegraphed to Oscar and Constance: 'Fear I may not be able to reach you in time. Don't wait.' 'We certainly shall not wait,' laughed Oscar as he prepared his buttonhole, 'neither shall we wait for the dear Queen. In this fine weather I asked her to remain at Osborne.'

Constance's grandfather was more than generous in his gifts to the couple. Having made them a wedding present of £5,000, which the couple used to purchase the lease of a house at 16 Tite Street, only a month after the ceremony he very considerately died, raising Constance's income to £900 per annum, and bringing the prospect of financial stability momentarily within the reach of her profligate husband.

Wilde asked Whistler if he would supervise the decoration of his new home, but Whistler refused assistance to his friend. 'No, Oscar,' he said, 'you have been lecturing to us about the House Beautiful; now is your chance to show us one.' After a fashion he did, but not in the fashion on which he had

*Oscar Wilde and Lord Alfred Douglas at the
beginning of their fatal friendship. Bosie reminded
a contemporary of 'a character from Shakespeare,'
but left us to speculate on which one.*

recently been lecturing. Instead he approached E.W. Godwin, the foremost of the æsthetic movement architects, who agreed to take on the job.

Sadly, not one single image appears to survive of any of the interiors that Wilde created and lived in; and it must be remembered that his collections of pictures, books and other objects, and even his furniture and personal effects were dispersed by the scandalously hurried sale of the contents of the Tite Street house following the bankruptcy immediately brought about by his trials in 1895. All his possessions remain tantalisingly obscure, other than by the meagre descriptions contained in the very inadequate catalogue prepared in a great rush by the auctioneers.

A certain amount has been written about the schemes that Wilde, with the help of Godwin, contrived for the house in Tite Street. Most accounts concentrate on the daring use of all-white enamelled woodwork and furnishings, and on the remarkable level of stylization of the interiors; as a result of these factors, Wilde's rooms certainly intrigued visitors and journalists alike. W.B.Yeats, invited by Oscar and Constance to spend Christmas Day of 1888 with them, was both fascinated and not a little intimidated by the rigorously artistic effects, such as the way in which a red lamp-

Whistler's famous Peacock Room, *now installed at the Smithsonian Institution in Washington. Wilde asked Whistler to supervise the decoration of his new home at Tite Street. He refused.*

shade hung over a small terracotta classical figure standing on a matching square of red cloth on the otherwise pristine white table.

This impression of extreme chic is, however, somewhat dispelled by the rather contrary evidence of the sale catalogue. From the admittedly sketchy descriptions of the contents of the house room by room, the objects listed suggest that the general effect may very well have been more that of a conventional family home of the 1880s or 90s, simply overlayed with some of the 'artistic' decorative ideas of the æsthetic movement, such as the use of oriental matting as a background to Persian carpets strewn across the floor. Clearly, Wilde's taste in Japonisme, when translated into the purchase of actual objects, lacked the finesse and sure æsthetic discrimination of either Rossetti or Whistler, and the feeling persists that Godwin's clever touches were in general grounded with, on the one hand, more prosaic or homely touches, and on the other with a hint of the commonplace, or at least the somewhat commercialised orientalism of Liberty's Bazaar. Wilde's splendour was one of phrases, not of visual effects.

Mr and Mrs Wilde left immediately to honeymoon in Paris – where they went several times to see Sarah Bernhardt as Lady Macbeth, and were entertained by John Singer Sargent, shortly to be a neighbour in Tite Street – and Dieppe, where they entertained themselves.

Two weeks before their arrival a book by J.K. Huysmans, a young disciple of Zola, was published in Paris, a work that was to have a profound influence on Wilde's life. *À Rebours*, translated variously as *In Revolt* or, more to the point, *Against Nature*, tells the story of the Duc Jean des Esseintes who, bored and disgusted by his fellow creatures, retreats from society; it anatomizes his search through ever more obscure paths for ever more refined and exquisite pleasures.

The book, which is in some ways the Gallic epitome of the Paterian æsthetical standpoint, was famously described by poet Arthur Symons as 'the Breviary of the Decadence'. Wilde, in *The Picture of Dorian Gray*, has Lord Henry Wotton refer to it as 'the strangest book he had ever read'; it contained all 'the sins of the world', and he reflects that 'the heavy odour of incense hung about its pages'.

For the whole generation of nineties dandy-æsthetes, the book had an extraordinary cult status and the hero came to be an iconic figure for Wilde in particular; the dark habits and secret vices cultivated for ostensibly scientific experiment by des Esseintes, were to be seen by Oscar reflected in his own private life in the coming years.

Oscar Wilde is in some ways as famous for his flamboyant dandyism as for his *belles-lettres*, but, while he owned essayist Thomas Carlyle's desk and thought it aided his inspiration, his approach to clothes was a more subtle affair than that satirised by Carlyle in his *Sartor Resartus*.

Wilde eventually dismissed his once cherished velvets and knee-breeches, telling Sherard, 'All that belonged to the Oscar of the first period. We are now concerned with the Oscar Wilde of the second period, who has nothing whatever in common with the gentleman who wore long hair and carried a sunflower down Piccadilly.' The costumes he paraded for his British audiences were a development of the literary dandyism he had discovered in Paris, quieted slightly so as not to frighten the provincial horses; although certainly unconventional, they were never those *outré* pantomimeries that the provinces had been given to expect.

A photograph taken while he lectured in the Isle of Wight in 1885 comes as something of a surprise given the image of the refined exquisite that emerges from Wilde's writings. Leaning away from the camera in a pose that has the unfortunate effect of exaggerating his physical size, the famous æsthete sports a white double-breasted reefer-suit, badly cut and badly fitting, his hair is cut in a longer version of the 'Neronian' curls he had adopted in Paris, and his hand cradles a tiny, dandified walking-stick and a large, battered wide-awake hat. 'The only connection between art and nature is in a really well-made buttonhole,' he once opined – the buttonhole here resembles a cabbage, the *tout ensemble* aimed at an unlikely cross between the gamin and the *louche* such as even Lord Alfred Douglas at the height of his youthful precocity would not have dared. And these were the days when Oscar Wilde stalked society preaching Dress Reform.

Thankfully, Wilde's dandyism became less exaggerated as he grew in maturity. As he sobered, Constance, like Lillie Langtry before her, became the peg on which Oscar hung his æsthetical manifesto. Although Lillie had eventually tired of her admirer's enthusiasms, Wilde's wife was not in so fortunate a position. Her wedding dress, designed by her fiancé, was described as of 'a delicate cowslip tint; the bodice finished with a high Medici collar; the skirt, made plain, was gathered by a silver girdle of beautiful workmanship, the gift of Mr Oscar Wilde', a saffron gauze veil thrown over all. The groom, confronted with such an image of decadent tastelessness, restrained himself in black.

A major element of Oscar's Dress Reform platform was the revival of a historical costumery no less ugly than that of his day, but less susceptible to the dictates of the hour. 'A fashion is merely a form of ugliness so unbearable that we are compelled to alter it every six months,' he was to write. In *Intentions*, Wilde set out his attitude to 'period' styles: 'we should never aim at any reconstruction of the past, nor burden ourselves with any fanciful necessity for historical accuracy. All beautiful things belong to the same age.' As Max Beerbohm amusingly put it: 'I, too, have my Elizabethan, my Caroline moments; I have gone to bed Georgian, and awoken early Victorian; even savagery has charmed me.' Max, though, had been spared the sight of Oscar at the height of his historical period.

Constance was tricked out in every style her husband's researches and imagination could devise. When the Wildes were presented to the Queen in 1887, they wore, in tribute to Her Majesty's Golden Jubilee, exact copies of the fashions of the coronation year. Such mummery was acceptable for a man like Wilde, whose dandyism naturally leaned towards a d'Orsay flashiness, but it must have been a strain for poor Constance. In a dress of 'limp white muslin with no bustle, saffron coloured silk swathed about her shoulders, a huge cartwheel Gainsborough hat, white and bright-yellow stockings and shoes' she earned the scorn of one friend. If she felt self-conscious in such trumpery, she showed it, 'she looked too hopeless, and we thought her shy and dull', continues the writer, who concludes, 'Oscar was amusing of course.' Perhaps he was laughing at his wife.

Wilde gradually left off his enthusiasm for both public and private lecturing. The hobby-horse of Dress Reform was put away and forgotten. By the mid-nineties his clothes were still exquisite, but ultra-fashionable, cut by the best tailors of the best broadcloth. The subtle skills of Savile Row's finest cutters became vitally important, for Wilde started to gain weight, and he shared his mother's vanity.

CHAPTER THREE

Feasting with Panthers

'**W**HY DO YOU ALWAYS WRITE POETRY?** *Pater had asked his student in 1877, 'Why do you not write prose? Prose is so much more difficult.' The truth of Pater's words did not sink in for some time. Oscar's first sustained attempt was a long essay entitled the 'Rise of Historical Criticism', written while trying to obtain an Oxford fellowship. Although an admirable piece of scholarship, it need not detain any but the most dedicated of his readers. It was not followed until 1885, with an article called 'Shakespeare and Stage Costume'. This, too, is a worthy and erudite treatise, but largely absent from it is that sparkle that we associate with Wilde's writing at the height of his powers.*

ABOVE: *Punch's representation of Oscar Wilde's speech to the first night audience of* Lady Windermere's Fan, *which was hailed by critics as 'the Champagne of literature'.*

RIGHT: *The Isle of Wight 1885, unsuccessfully trying to conceal the results of habitual excess.*

The dandy *flâneur* of London and Paris used to insist that 'work is for those who have nothing better to do', but the year after his marriage, with little money coming into the household and its profligate master distributing borrowed guineas as if he were sowing a field, the old financial worries were again apparent. Constance had been so concerned about the couple's financial prospects that on their return from honeymoon she proposed taking up employment herself. Before this could happen, and before the decorations at Tite Street had allowed them to move in, Constance fell pregnant with her first child in September 1884.

The soon-to-be paterfamilias was forced to support his family, and an always uneasy friendship with W.E. Henley at the *Pall Mall Gazette* secured him a position reviewing books for the paper that had only recently been enthusiastically joining in the public mockery of the æsthete.

'I am never disappointed in literary men,' Wilde told Edmund Gosse when the writer had admitted to nervousness about meeting Wilde, 'I think they are perfectly charming. It is their works I find so disappointing.' In his reviews for the *Gazette* are to be found some of the best writing Oscar ever did. Since the paper did not give its contributors bylines, he was forced to distinguish himself by means of style alone. His pieces are always well – sometimes brilliantly – written. Rarely turning in anything that was not just on the right side of overwritten, he never allowed himself to be cowed by the lustre of an author's name, or lulled by the dullness of his prose.

'Ours,' he wrote of one of the hundreds of novels sent to him 'may be a prosaic age, but we fear that it is not an age of prose.' Despite an unbendingly hostile attitude to the workaday and the dull he usually contrived to leaven his criticism – even of the worst production – with a note of kindness or encouragement, for he realized the use both to the writer and to himself of an appreciative quote in publishers' advertisements. And although he could be at times brusque, and even apparently rude, Wilde genuinely never liked to hurt people's feelings.

From the dreariness of most of the books he reviewed between 1885 and 1890, Oscar Wilde realised an overriding truth, one which his own age had forgotten in its fear of anarchy, and hatred of the Georgians: 'It is a curious fact that the worst work is always done with the best intentions, and that people are never so trivial as when they take themselves seriously.' Henceforth, the serious high-mindedness that had elicited *Vera* and *The Duchess of Padua* was to be banished in favour of a highly polished lightness of touch that has, at its best, few equals.

Oscar and Constance were blissfully happy for the first few years of their marriage. Living in a succession of stop-gaps until the decorations at Tite Street were finished had forced them into each other's pockets, yet they displayed all evidence of nuptial bliss. In the first months Oscar's affection was so great that he habitually accompanied his wife on shopping expeditions, and when parted from her rarely returned without bringing flowers, gifts or other tokens of his love. During her first pregnancy his devotion cooled slightly, but after Constance's confinement and the birth in the summer of 1885 of Cyril, the first of their two sons, the couple started to go out together again, and outwardly seemed as much in love as before.

With Vyvyan's birth in the next year, however, Constance began to tire of her husband's carelessness, levity and irresponsibility. She would, at the luncheons they regularly gave, interrupt Oscar's flights of fancy with mundane reminders of the various chores and tasks he had forgotten; gradually Oscar began to look for diversion – and, in due course, affection – elsewhere.

Impressed by his work at the *Pall Mall Gazette*, in June 1887 the directors of Cassell and Co asked Wilde to take over as editor of the *Lady's World*, a magazine until then directed to the more ambitious suburban housewife. Under Wilde's editorship its character was to change for the better. His first executive act was to change the name to *Woman's World*, a rechristening that at a stroke removed the associations the old title had with bas-bourgeois snobbery and reflected his advanced views on female emancipation.

The mast-head of the Woman's World. *Having successfully avoided yellow fever in America, Oscar had no fear of yellow journalism.*

In the first flush of enthusiasm for his new job he managed to entice contributions not only from good writers, but famous personalities. The Queen of Romania, Princess Christian and Marie Corelli all wrote articles. Queen Victoria, however, despite having recently had her *More Leaves from a Highland Journal* published, firmly refused Wilde's reverent request for permission to print her early poems. 'Really, what will people not say and invent,' Her Imperial Majesty wrote in a memorandum, 'Never could the Queen in her whole life write one line of poetry serious or comic or make a rhyme ever.' All in all though, the Queen seemed rather pleased by the request.

Sarah Bernhardt was commissioned to elucidate 'The History of my Tea-Gown' and Wilde also suggested to the actress an article reminiscing on her own recently concluded American tour. Going so far as to offer to write the piece himself, in his letter Oscar expressed his profound respect for the French nation's tolerance of Americans coming to Europe to complete the education of their offspring: Americans were, he quipped, 'people who are so fascinatingly unreasonable as to attempt to finish in a foreign land what they never had the courage to begin in their own'.

With only modest means, this was not the time for Oscar to be wafted about London in gilded taxi-carriages. On the contrary, he travelled to Cassell's offices in Ludgate Hill by the newly constructed underground railway, boarding at Sloane Square and debouching at Charing Cross, to walk the rest of the way to the City. Always said to have been the best-dressed man in the Square Mile, at eleven in the morning the competition from fellow dandies could at that hour – or in that locale – not have been stiff. And while the appointed hour of eleven might at first have found him at the office, his arrival tended to slip further and further into the reaches of the afternoon, so that too often he would only get there just in time to leave for luncheon.

In truth, Wilde was keen to lose such regular employment, for as his intellectual power improved, he knew his talents to be wasted in the more polite quarters of Grub Street. The column of literary notes he was engaged to write, for example, actually appeared in only ten of the twenty-odd editions he edited, and many of those were composed by his admiring colleagues. 'So indolent,' sighed one of Cassell's directors, 'but such a genius.'

Wilde's stratagem of infuriating his own superiors at the publishing house by blatant idleness was augmented by an early resolution never to answer their summonses. As he told Henley, 'I have known men come to London full of bright prospects and seen them complete wrecks a few months later through a habit of answering letters.' The prestige of displaying the name of Oscar Wilde on the pink mast-head of the *Woman's World* was, however, too great for Cassell's to drop its star in a hurry, and his tenure lasted more than two years, by which time his latent genius could no longer remain hidden under the carefully assumed pose of laconic idleness. In fact, the late 1880s were, by sheer volume, Wilde's most productive period, the time in which, having worked out his apprenticeship in letters, he emerged as a individual writer of immense talent.

Robert Sherard described Wilde's conversation as 'the most wonderful things said in the golden voice of the most wonderful woman. To have heard him speak has made the fortune of innumerable little men. The smallest change from his royal storehouse has made hundreds appear rich. Out of the tatters of his imperial mantle, which disaster dragged in the mire, many writers, many speakers, have cut for them-selves resplendent robes in which they strut their small parades and enjoy their tiny triumphs'.

Oscar's almost miraculous conversational gifts have led him to be looked on as the greatest of a great tradition of British wits. The fable he once embroidered about a gathering of sentient iron-filings, ineluctably drawn towards a nearby magnet, all the while believing that it is their own free will that attracts them there, could have been autobiographical. His flights of anecdotal genius would begin in private conversations with one or two of a gathering; one by one, drawn by the uproarious laughter emanating from his end of the table, the entire company would gradually fall silent to experience the magnificence of his eloquence.

Much of his raconteur's magic lay in such fables, which he was ever inventing, fining and refining in his talk, and the stories that eventually found their way into print were often only the most pared-down treatments of these conversational *tours de force*. Urged by admiring listeners to publish his tales, he would always profess to be unequal to raising the energy required to write them down; yet for the February 1887 issue of *The Court and Society Review* he was enticed to complete his first major work of fiction, 'The Canterville Ghost', his famously amusing story about a ghost that attempts to haunt a parvenu American family out of an ancestral English home.

Wilde's growing fascination with sin and fate is evident in 'Lord Arthur Savile's Crime', published later that year in the same pages, and 1888 saw these stories published in a collection of gently ironic short fables, ostensibly for children, but written just as much to amuse adult readers, entitled *The Happy Prince and Other Tales*. The other tales included 'The Selfish Giant', one of his most popular works, and 'The Remarkable Rocket', in which a self-important firework – a caricature of Whistler – signally fails to live up to his self-advertisement. Spluttering out in a puddle, unseen by the world, the rocket exclaims: 'There, I knew I would cause a sensation.'

Like his edition of *Poems*, the volume was 'charmingly got up', and although no lambent example of the typographer's art, it did boast drawings by Walter Crane, the pre-eminent illustrator of children's books of the day. The possibilities for really original book design were not fully brought home to Wilde until he was sent, in 1889, the first number of an artistic magazine called *The Dial*, designed by two young artists, Charles Ricketts and Charles Shannon. *The Dial* was a precocious show-piece of avant-garde design, remarkable no less for its advanced literary content than its startling layout and use of type. Half facetiously, in the note he sent to acknowledge their gift, Wilde advised them to print no further editions: 'All perfect things should be unique'.

Although the two artists lived at No 1, The Vale, a Chelsea house recently vacated by Whistler, Ricketts's personal dislike of the painter was guaranteed to amuse Wilde, while their collection of *objets de vertu*, old master drawings, Japanese prints, rare and fantastic shells and Greek antiquities provided an atmosphere of unusually intense æstheticism. Here, it was always claimed, Wilde was at his best as a talker, but in the atmosphere of deliberately rarefied taste and learning, the informal evenings of modest food, plentiful wine and rich conversation which made The Vale, as he used to say 'The one house in London where you will never be bored,' he also became that *rara avis*, a good listener.

Just as Wilde had once deferred to Whistler's artistic judgements, in turn he came to regard Ricketts, although ten years his junior, as his æsthetic mentor. Ricketts and Shannon became 'official

Jeffrey Lenz in the 1996 production of Lowell Liebermann's
The Picture of Dorian Gray, *directed by John Cox at the*
Opéra de Monte Carlo. Dorian Gray was published in the
summer of 1891. The outcry was delicious.

artists to Oscar Wilde'. All the books he published before his fall, with the exception of John Lane's edition of *Salome*, designed by the precociously brilliant Aubrey Beardsley, were designed, or 'pictured', as Wilde preferred to term it, by the two men. Their radical achievement on *The Dial* had persuaded him that the 'Book Beautiful' was as worthy and realistic a conception as the 'House Beautiful'.

Their first effort, another book of fables, *A House of Pomegranates*, of 1891, was a qualified success, but their best collaboration came in 1894, on *The Sphinx*, a poem on which Wilde had been sporadically working since the 1870s. The splendour of Wilde's text, which brings into play a rich and sonorous poetic lexicon of ancient myth, precious stones and the world of desert saints, was precisely mirrored by the luxury of Ricketts's vellum binding, while its essential weirdness found its echo in his typography. Set in small capitals with green initial letters, with its asymmetric layouts and illustrations printed in red ink, *The Sphinx* is unquestionably the most beautiful book of the century, and one of the quintessential expressions of the rarefied sensibilities of the 1890s.

The first of Oscar's highly successful duologues, 'The Decay of Lying', was published in January 1889, and was followed the next year by 'The Critic as Artist'. The literary form he chose, invented by the Greeks but largely ignored since the seventeenth century, was a liberating discovery, for it allowed him to set up in prose the paradoxes that were always the chief ornaments of his conversation.

His philosophical positions are set out by two languid dandies, and the eminently cogent trains of thought are thus given a light style which makes them the most readable of ethical treatises, entirely lacking in the atmosphere of bombast from which straightforwardly treated moral works generally suffer. In 1891 the essays were collected with the old 'Truth of Masks' article and a new piece entitled 'Pen, Pencil and Poison', in a volume called *Intentions*.

In 'Pen, Pencil and Poison', the writer at his capricious best, Wilde turns his gaze upon the Regency art critic, journalist, forger, and 'subtle secret poisoner almost without rival', Thomas Griffiths Wainewright. Far from taking Wainewright to task for the gratuitous murders of several members of his family, Wilde chooses only to praise the dandy's refined artistic sensibilities. 'The fact,' as he put it, 'of a man being poisoner is nothing against his prose. The domestic virtues are not the true basis of art.'

The publication of *Intentions* marks a major step in Wilde's own attempt to, like Baudelaire, bring 'every complication of taste, the exasperation of perfumes, the irritant of cruelty, the very odours and colours of corruption to the creation of a sort of religion in which an eternal mass is served before a veiled altar'. That new sort of religion, a religion of Beauty was, of course, to be identified with a new sort of art; an art that had as its object 'not simple truth, but complex beauty'.

The Picture of Dorian Gray, the book which for many readers functions as the most exquisite flower of decadence, was commissioned at the same time as Sir Arthur Conan Doyle's second Sherlock Holmes story, *The Sign of Four*, and published in *Lippincott's Magazine* in July 1890.

Aubrey Beardsley

RIGHT: *Jaques-Emile Blanche's portrait of the artist Aubrey Beardsley: his face 'like a silver hatchet'.*

LEFT *and* RIGHT: *Two of Beardsley's designs for Wilde's Salome, at least as faithful to the text as Lord Alfred Douglas's translation.*

TOP LEFT: *'The Entrance of Herodias' from* Salome *with Wilde caricatured as her Fool.*

BOTTOM LEFT: *Frontispiece to John Davidson's* Plays; *Wilde appears 'with vine leaves in his hair'.*

BELOW: The Peacock Skirt, *from Salome.*

In Wilde's story, the painter Basil Hallward becomes obsessed with the extraordinary beauty of the young man-about-town, Dorian Gray, and paints his portrait. Dorian's suavely cynical mentor Lord Henry Wotton persuades him that the only real virtues in life are youth and beauty, and in a moment of despair at the thought of losing his beauty through ageing, Dorian prays that his portrait may grow old, while he himself should remain forever young and beautiful.

His prayer is answered, and the ensuing narrative presents the anatomy of Huysmans' and Pater's æsthetic philosophies. Gray goes about London ruining lives and reputations; he engages in nameless vices and loathsome practices, and while his portrait reflects the increasingly foul corruption of his soul, his own appearance remains unaffected. Finally, tired of the evil of his life, and hoping to repair some of the damage he has done, Dorian commits a good deed, but when he returns to examine the mirror of his soul, he finds only that a look of unutterable hypocrisy is now reflected in the portrait.

Enraged, he tries to destroy it, using the knife with which he had killed the painter Basil Hallward, but himself dies from the knife's thrust. His servants, investigating a noise in the attic where Dorian kept the portrait, find 'a dead man in evening dress, with a knife in his heart. He was withered, wrinkled, and loathsome of visage. It was not until they had examined the rings that they recognized who it was'. The portrait had regained its former sweetness and beauty.

Though the story is in places thematically inconclusive, it was not for its stylistic imperfections that the newspapers variously seized upon the work as 'disgusting', 'stupid and vulgar', or even 'unmanly, sickening, vicious and tedious'. Indeed, in their wrath and indignation that a work of such patent immorality could be perpetrated on the British public, they left it to later critics to realize how imperfectly constructed the story is; nor does their dismissal explain how, despite its various faults, the book remains even today one of Wilde's best and most popular works.

'A publicist is a man who bores the community with the illegalities of his private life,' Wilde had written about Wainewright. Although in *The Picture of Dorian Gray* Wilde was careful to veil the specific details of his hero's secret vices, it required no great textual analyst to divine what they were. The *Scots Observer*, for one, had no trouble, and making an unmistakable reference to the recent 'Cleveland Street' homosexual scandal, in which a network of rent-boys and their aristocratic clients had been discovered in Covent Garden, the newspaper wrote: 'If Mr Wilde can write for none but outlawed noblemen and perverted telegraph boys, the sooner he takes to tailoring (or some other decent trade) the better for his own reputation and the public morals.'

The Picture of Dorian Gray was published in book form in the early summer of 1891, and Wilde made sure of its continued notoriety by adding a Preface of flippant maxims on art. Greeted by another chorus of outraged publicity, when W.H. Smith and Sons refused to stock the volume on the grounds of its questionable morality, the first edition was guaranteed to sell out.

But *Dorian Gray* mortally shocked the reading public, and where once its author had been laughed at by the respectable, he now met more open enmity; he was blackballed from a West End club, and, as he had described the treatment meted out to Dorian, in an example of life imitating fiction, men would pointedly leave the room when he entered.

※ ※ ※

In 1885, Oscar was invited to see an undergraduate performance of the *Euminides* at Cambridge. The perhaps fateful invitation had come from Harry Marillier, who had lodged, whilst a Bluecoat schoolboy, in Wilde's house at Salisbury Street. Oscar became infatuated by the boy who had once brought him matutinal cups of coffee, and soon passionate letters were being exchanged between them. Their relationship never developed into a physical intimacy, however, and although they always remained close, Oscar's affections devolved upon successive members of Marillier's set.

Among the Cambridge undergraduates to whom Marillier introduced him, Wilde was treated like a hero. 'I like people who are young, bright, happy, careless and original,' Wilde was to declare later at his trial, 'I do not like them sensible, and I do not like them old.' He was invigorated by the honest, straightforward enthusiasm of these young men, and through them he felt that he had rediscovered the noble platonic ideal of intense masculine friendship. '"The love that dare not speak its name" in this century,' Oscar was to say at his trial, 'is such a great affection as Plato made the very basis of his philosophy, and such as you find in the sonnets of Michelangelo and Shakespeare. It is that deep, spiritual affection that is as pure as it is perfect. It is in this century misunderstood.'

By Wilde's own account, it was not until he met in 1886 a young man named Robbie Ross, the son of a Canadian Attorney-General, that he was to know physical love between men. 'Little Robbie' the sensitive boy with 'the face of Puck' was an athlete who rowed for his college, and at the same time an æsthete who received the traditional ducking meted out by the bloods to anyone suspected of artistic leanings; his character was, according to the mood of his companions, alternately gravely attentive or

Oscar Wilde, who used to sit up all night with withering flowers for fear they might die alone, caricatured by Punch.

When George Alexander asked for a play to produce, he was
offered The Duchess of Padua, *but wisely refused it. Instead*
Oscar wrote Lady Windermere's Fan.

else irrepressibly enthusiastic. Although only distantly, Wilde had been his idol for some years, and as a boy he had been thrashed for reading Wilde's *Poems*.

As openly homosexual as it was possible to be in those days, Ross set out to seduce his poet, and although their affair did not last long, Ross certainly provided Wilde's first heady introduction to the London homosexual underworld. The future author of *Dorian Gray* was fascinated by the underbelly of Victorian England, which Robbie – highly experienced despite his youth – guided him through, and after their dalliance was over, Ross would remain always Wilde's most devoted, most loyal, and most unselfish friend, while Oscar continued his – ever tentative – explorations of forbidden passions.

Sheridan was one of a select few whose writing even approaches their conversational reputations, and Wilde's genius is often compared to that of the Georgian playwright whose passion for the stage had led him to buy the Drury Lane Theatre. In truth, they shared more than a literary genius. Fate did not intend for 'Sherry' long to enjoy his possession, and soon the theatre burnt down. In the middle of the conflagration, the owner was discovered drinking in a tavern across the street. When someone approached him, expressing amazement at his coolness in the face of his ruin: Sheridan replied, 'A man may take a glass of beer by his own fire-side, may he not?' Oscar was to show a similar determined resignation when his own fate eventually caught up with him.

Probably after a Café Royal lunch, entranced by some tale Oscar had sketched for the amusement of his listeners, George Alexander, who had just taken over as actor-manager of the St James's Theatre, begged Wilde to write him a play. The proffered advance of £100 Wilde simply trousered, and wrote nothing. Although his early drama *The Duchess of Padua* was being revived in New York – to some acclaim – under the title of *Guido Ferranti*, in the midst of the furore over *Dorian Gray*, Wilde was in no mood to put his head above the parapet for now.

Alexander was not easily put off, and his tempting promises of vast profits and popular acclaim eventually inspired the writer to action. In less than a month during the autumn of 1891, Wilde wrote *Lady Windermere's Fan*, his first comedy. The quality of Wilde's writing exceeded all Alexander's expectations, and he offered to buy the rights for the unheard-of sum of £1,000. Oscar thought better of the work he had dismissed as 'one of those modern drawing-room plays with pink lampshades': 'I have so much confidence in your excellent judgement, my dear Alec,' he said, 'that I cannot but refuse your generous offer. I will take a percentage.'

With the play about to go into production, as the 'Oscar of the first period' had, after the success of his American lecture tour, made a splash in Paris so the Oscar of the third period, England's most talked-of writer, turned his attention again to the conquest of France. This time, too, he took with him copies of his new book, but now Wilde needed no letters of introduction. *L'Echo de Paris* heralded his arrival as 'le "great event"' of literary Paris of 1891.

Whistler, now living in the city, did his best to spoil his old rival's welcome, but Wilde's charm was enough, for the most part, to counteract the painter's malice at the salons of poets like Mallarmé and Jean Moréas. Other new friends included the Symbolist poet Marcel Schwob, who was to translate much of Wilde's work into French; Catulle Mendès, who was later to deny having known Wilde, and fought a duel to assert the truth of his dishonest denial; and a young writer called Pierre Louÿs, who was beginning to make a name for himself as a Greek scholar *extraordinaire* and the writer of verses of unsurpassed febrility.

Inspired by the Symbolists, Wilde began to write, in French, *Salome*, his strangest, and probably his worst, literary work. A treatment of the biblical story of John the Baptist and Herodias's daughter, Oscar's interest in the theme pre-dated his arrival in Paris, but the devotion Mallarmé inspired amongst his followers seems to have drawn the master of English letters to compete with the Maître, while Sarah Bernhardt's willingness to take the leading role only served to encourage Wilde in his high regard for the play.

Wilde's version of the tale has the same perfumed unreality and overpowering sensuality that pervades the French literature of this period. With its slow, repetitive and emphatic speeches, its poetic diction, and obsessive building of word-pictures, in *Salome* Wilde comes closer than any other English writer of his period to the precious, decadent hothouse style of contemporary European writing.

Salome completed, Oscar returned to London in January, to oversee rehearsals of *Lady Windermere's Fan*, which opened at Alexander's St. James's Theatre on 20 February 1892. He met his friend Graham Robertson the day before, and the artist recalled that Wilde asked him to wear a green carnation in his buttonhole at the première. 'I want a lot of men to wear them,' he explained, 'it will annoy the public.'

'But why annoy the public?' asked Robertson.

'It likes to be annoyed.'

Wilde explained that the actor playing Cecil Graham, a proto-Wildean character, would also be wearing this weird bloom, and, when the audience examined its own ranks, it would find, scattered 'here and there, more and more mystic specks of green. "This must be some secret symbol," they will say, "what on earth can it mean?"'

'And what does it mean?' asked Robertson.

'Nothing whatever,' came the reply, 'but that is just what nobody will guess.'

The audience's appreciation of Wilde's dark and penetratingly funny play lived up to all Alexander's predictions. In response to deafening calls of 'Author' as the curtain fell, Wilde stepped from the wings, in his hand a lighted gold-tipped cigarette. His short speech was a masterpiece of dandified bravado and impudence, calculated to *épater les bourgeois*.

'Ladies and Gentlemen,' he said, 'I have enjoyed this evening immensely. The actors have given us a charming rendition of a delightful play, and your appreciation has been most intelligent. I congratulate you on the great success of your performance, which persuades me that you think almost as highly of the play as I do myself.'

If anything, his nonchalance increased the public's admiration for his wit and cleverness, but the casual insolence of the words and the gesture particularly offended the dramatic critics. Incensed by his manner, jealously irritated by his talent, enraged by his popularity, they, almost to a man, disparaged the play and its author. None seemed to notice the carnations.

Some of *Lady Windermere's* audience would have known very well, and many more might have guessed, the secret symbolism of these badges of decadence. However, Robertson was not entirely naïve

Theatre programme for Lady Windermere's Fan,
Oscar Wilde's first dramatic success. Originally called
A Good Woman, *the title was changed when Lady*
Wilde suggested it was not sufficiently obscure.

to express his ignorance of the meaning of a flower that was so clearly *à rebours*, for the secret of Wilde's increasingly active homosexual life was not generally known, even to close friends like Frank Harris, editor of the *Saturday Review*.

We would now define Oscar's pose of effeminacy, which so many people in both Paris and London noticed and commented upon, as 'camp', but in his time it was assumed to be part of the æsthetic pose he so amusingly cultivated. When the character of Cecil Graham says in *Lady Windermere* that 'nothing looks so like innocence as indiscretion', Wilde was reflecting society's assumptions about him. No one would so openly defy convention as he was now doing if there were any cause for concern: society presumed that Oscar's 'unmanliness', like his impudence, was merely designed to shock them, and for now, while he was amusing it, society did not care to look behind his mask.

Referring to the three characters he had created in *The Picture of Dorian Gray*, Wilde declared, 'Basil Hallward is what I think I am; Lord Henry what the world thinks me; Dorian is what I would like to be.' In June 1891, a little while after the book publication of *Dorian Gray*, he was approached by Lord Alfred Douglas, the youngest son of the Marquess of Queensberry, from whom Dorian's description might have been directly taken.

'Bosie', the name by which his family knew him, an alabaster pale, blond-haired twenty-one year old up at Magdalen, gushed that he had read *Dorian Gray* 'fourteen times running' in the wildest admiration. Oscar was flattered, and more than a little attracted, and, learning that Douglas was struggling with the classics at his old college, offered to help Bosie with tuition.

The history of Lord Alfred Douglas's family is old and colourful. Descendant of the revolting 'Black Douglas' and of the lecherous 'Old Q' of the Regency, Bosie's father, the Ninth Marquess of Queensberry, was a militant atheist, expelled from the House of Lords for his anti-religious bigotry, whose passion for pugilism had led him, while still in his twenties, to regularize the rules of boxing, which carry his name today.

Bosie, his third and youngest son, was beautiful and amusing, young and spoiled; he was also reckless, arrogant and a spendthrift, with an almost insane pride and an uncontrollable temper which, like his father, he unleashed against anyone who stood between him and his pleasures. These qualities were deeply and perversely attractive to Wilde, but not the least interesting of all was Bosie's position as the scion of an old noble house.

RIGHT: *Edith Evans as Lady Bracknell*
in the 1952 film of Earnest. *'Never speak*
disrespectfully of Society. Only people
who can't get into it do that.'

Rather than return to domesticity at Tite Street, Oscar would often take a suite at the Savoy for the night, and when his private life became more unmanageable – staff at the hotel began to be suspicious of the young men they found in his bed in the mornings – he took a suite of bachelor's chambers in St James's, partly and ostensibly to write, but partly to conduct less publicly affairs, such as the one he was having with the poet John Gray at the time of his first acquaintance with Lord Alfred Douglas.

His marriage, though we are told his affection for his wife and love for his two young sons never left him, was, if not quite dead, then utterly changed. To explain his distance, he appears to have told Constance that the syphilis he had contracted at Oxford had reappeared, and Constance, occupied with Cyril and Vyvyan, the house and good causes, does not appear greatly to have resented her loss. From time to time they could still be seen in each other's company at parties; they continued to entertain together on occasion; he still designed bizarre costumes for her, but they had drifted apart.

The intimacy between Wilde and Douglas started gradually, but, in an eerie presage of what was in store, events early in 1892 brought them into close and conspiratorial contact. Bosie was being blackmailed over some indiscreet letters and came to Wilde for help. Oscar, by nature generous, but fascinated by Douglas's unblushing wickedness, gave him the money he needed to buy them back. By the middle of that year, Bosie had supplanted all others as Wilde's favourite.

Encouraged by Wilde, as John Gray and others had been before him, Bosie began to consider himself a poet, and upon the empty and superficial, but technically accomplished sonnets he wrote Wilde bestowed extravagant praise. Whether he believed his own praise is doubtful, for he later dismissed Bosie's work as 'of the undergraduate school of verse', but Oscar's patronage gave to Douglas a cachet that helped to secure some distinguished contributors for his undergraduate magazine, *The Spirit Lamp*. Here Max Beerbohm's first essay was published, as well as one of J.A. Symons's last. The Marquess of Queensberry, too, was persuaded to contribute. His poem, in an absurd echo of Christina Rossetti's more famous 'Song', began: 'When I am dead, cremate me.'

The playbill of Oscar's second play of modern life. 'The Book of Life begins with a man and woman in a garden. It ends with Revelations.'

The lines of influence were not all in one direction, however, and while Wilde shepherded Lord Alfred through the world of letters, Bosie took Oscar deeper into a milieu less refined, but more immediately stimulating. Increasingly during their relationship, Douglas brought recklessness to a fine art: he would never take the hazardous option if a suicidal one presented itself, and his attitude to sexual inter-course – wherever, whenever, whomever – and love of danger began to excite and entrance Wilde.

Although Robbie Ross had introduced Oscar, on occasions, to rough trade, the lower-class boys who made up the lowest rank of the underworld, Douglas had a friend able to provide an endless supply of such creatures, whose bodies – and even their souls – could be purchased for a pound and a meal. Alfred Taylor, an ex-public-school boy who had, by the age of thirty, squandered an inheritance of £45,000, ran a delicate and peculiar commercial service introducing gentlemen to their social inferiors from his rooms behind Westminster Abbey.

Wilde was fascinated by the inhabitants of Taylor's dangerous world. They 'were wonderful', he was to say of two of the dubious acquaintances he made there, 'in their

A portrait of Herbert Beerbohm Tree, whom Wilde regarded as the best critic of his plays, because he never wanted to impress his own personality on them.

infamous war against life. To know them was an astounding adventure'. But neither Taylor nor Wilde knew then that many of the boys had discovered for themselves a lucrative side-line in extortion, thanks to the Criminal Law Amendment Act of 1885, which, for the first time, had made all sexual acts between men illegal, and became known as the 'Blackmailer's Charter'.

For the moment, Wilde enjoyed, perhaps in genuine naïvety, the pleasures of seeking out exotic and novel pleasures according to Paterian principles. Paradoxically, his first brush with the law came not through his fascination with 'feasting with panthers', but as a result of his desire to bring to life Salome, his biblical *femme fatale*, on the English stage

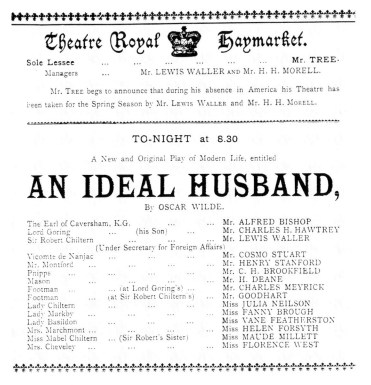

Theatre Royal ♛ Haymarket.

Sole Lessee ... ... Mr. TREE·
Managers ... Mr. LEWIS WALLER AND Mr. H. H. MORELL.

Mr. TREE begs to announce that during his absence in America his Theatre has been taken for the Spring Season by Mr. LEWIS WALLER and Mr. H. H. MORELL.

TO-NIGHT at 8.30

A New and Original Play of Modern Life, entitled

AN IDEAL HUSBAND,

By OSCAR WILDE.

The Earl of Caversham, K.G.	...	Mr. ALFRED BISHOP
Lord Goring ... (his Son) ...		Mr. CHARLES H. HAWTREY
Sir Robert Chiltern	...	Mr. LEWIS WALLER
(Under Secretary for Foreign Affairs)		
Vicomte de Nanjac		Mr. COSMO STUART
Mr. Montford	...	Mr. HENRY STANFORD
Phipps		Mr. C. H. BROOKFIELD
Mason		Mr. H. DEANE
Footman ... ... (at Lord Goring's) ...		Mr. CHARLES MEYRICK
Footman ... (at Sir Robert Chiltern's)		Mr. GOODHART
Lady Chiltern		Miss JULIA NEILSON
Lady Markby	...	Miss FANNY BROUGH
Lady Basildon		Miss VANE FEATHERSTON
Mrs. Marchmont	...	Miss HELEN FORSYTH
Miss Mabel Chiltern ... (Sir Robert's Sister)		Miss MAUDE MILLETT
Mrs. Cheveley	...	Miss FLORENCE WEST

A playbill for An Ideal Husband, *premièred in 1895. During rehearsals, Oscar made enemies of Charles Hawtrey and Charles Brookfield, who later played Judas to Wilde's Christ.*

With London at his feet, it seemed to Wilde, in the summer of 1893, that the time was right to stage a production of *Salome*, and he approached the fifty-year-old, increasingly rotund Sarah Bernhardt to take the role of the sixteen-year-old dancing princess. Bernhardt had taken the Palace Theatre for a season, and agreed immediately to Wilde's suggestion. The play was in the second week of rehearsals, and much money had been spent on sets by Ricketts, on costumes and on wages, when it was realized that Wilde had not obtained the necessary approval from the Lord Chancellor, whose duty it was to censor every dramatic production.

Permission was denied on a bizarre technicality: an obscure seventeenth-century anti-Catholic law prohibited the representation of biblical figures on the stage. Sarah Bernhardt was understandably furious with Oscar at the waste of time and money to which his irresponsibility had put her, and never really forgave him. Wilde was no less angry, and in an interview with the *Pall Mall Gazette* threatened to leave England. When someone pointed out that if he took up French nationality, he would have to do military service, he retreated: 'Well, my dear, that requires a lot of thought,' he said, and hastily dropped the idea.

Meanwhile, envious of the success George Alexander's supposedly inferior talents were enjoying in *Lady Windermere*, Herbert Beerbohm Tree, actor-manager at the Haymarket and a close friend of Wilde, tried to commission a similar comedy for himself. Wilde, though, was doubtful of Tree's suitability for a light comic role, and refused the request. 'As Herod in my *Salome* you would be admirable,' he told Tree. 'As a peer of the realm in my latest dramatic device, forgive me if I do not see you.'

But, having been right in his judgement of Alexander's acumen – *Lady Windermere* eventually brought him more than £7,000 – the prospect of another such hit was understandably attractive. Consequently, the early summer of 1892 found Wilde at a borrowed house in Torquay, writing *A Woman of No Importance*. It premièred in April 1893, and was received with as much, if not more, adulation as its predecessor had been. The wicked Lord Illingworth, in particular, thrilled the audience, who discerned in the character something of its author's self-portrait, and adored the dangerous charm Tree brought to the role for which he considered himself made.

It need hardly be stated that the press reviews of the play were less adulatory, but, for the first time, august newspapers like *The Times* showed themselves willing to judge the work on its own merits. 'The play is fresh in its ideas and executions,' wrote its critic, 'and is moreover written with a literary polish too rare on the English stage.' The Prince of Wales agreed, advising, 'Do not change a line'.

Basking in his success, and almost overwhelmed by the vast income brought by two consecutive theatrical hits, Wilde set about enjoying his fame. He found a new role as Mæcenas, and drew about himself a crowd of poets, writers, painters and mere bon viveurs, who gave him, in return for loans and gifts of money, for lunches at the Café Royal and dinners at the Savoy or Kettners, the adulation he had so long desired.

Now, with all financial pressures at last removed, Wilde was able to indulge to the fullest his love of luxury for luxury's sake. He had taxi-cabs on semi-permanent hire, and would pay well over the odds for items large or small, merely for the joy of watching money slip through his fingers, knowing that there was always more to replace it. On one occasion, sending for a packet of the expensive gold-tipped cigarettes which he was rarely without, he was told that there were none available. Handing over a guinea for an inferior packet, he dismissed the change when the waiter offered it to him, saying: 'No, keep it. That way I'll delude myself into thinking these are good.'

Charles Hawtrey as Lord Goring in An Ideal Husband. *'If there was less sympathy in the world there would be less trouble.'*

The quixotic generosity with which he treated his general circle was lavished in particular on Lord Alfred Douglas, from whom he was now practically inseparable. For almost all of 1893 they were rarely out of each other's company, and it is not surprising, given his assertion in *De Profundis* that he never wrote a line when in Douglas's company, that in that year he produced almost no new work.

When Lord Alfred had gone up to Oxford in 1891, the Marquess of Queensberry was genuinely proud of his son, but the boy was not made for scholastic application – or filial piety. His main interests were high life and horse racing, and he soon drew down upon himself the ire of an anyway irascible father for his dissolute and profligate lifestyle. As Wilde and Bosie became closer, both Lord and Lady Queensberry began to worry about their intimacy, he because he scented unmanliness, she because she feared that Wilde would act the role of Lord Henry Wotton to Bosie's Dorian Gray. She did not realize the true position was quite the reverse.

It would be difficult to put a cigarette paper between the volatile and incendiary characters of Bosie and his father, and a conflict between them – which in most families would have taken years to come to full fruition – exploded into a violent feud almost immediately. But Bosie had one ordnance in his armament not available to his father: manipulation. Realizing that Oscar could be used as both a weapon and a shield against his father, he began to place Wilde, in Frank Harris's memorable phrase, 'between the wood and the bark'.

The family quarrel became more heated in the summer of 1893, after Bosie failed to turn up for his examinations, and was thrown out of Oxford: this, felt the Marquess, was the result of Wilde's bad influence on his son. It was made worse when at the end on the year, to forestall a scandal involving a schoolboy, indiscreet letters and misspent nights, Bosie was forced to flee to Egypt.

In the spring of 1893, Robbie Ross had pointed Wilde's attention to an illustration in *The Studio*, a new art journal. It was a drawing of Salome, holding by the hair the severed head of John the Baptist, and was the work of Aubrey Beardsley, a young artist whose illustrated edition of Malory's *Morte D'Arthur* was about to be published by J.M. Dent. A French edition of *Salome* had been published in February, but without illustrations, and sensing potential celebrity and sales, the publisher John Lane readily agreed to an English edition. Beardsley seemed the only choice for the illustrator, and it only remained to arrange for a translation of the text.

Why Oscar did not do the translation himself is not clear, but whether as the result of the subtle emotional coercion at which he was so good, or to help confer on him a reputation for *belles-lettres*, Bosie was commissioned to undertake the project. He started in May, and had delivered his translation by the end of August; only then did Wilde discover that his protégé had but the slightest acquaintance with the French language. Whole passages had been mistranslated, which, given the nature of the text, might not irremediably have marred the effect had not Bosie refused, when his errors were pointed out, to change a line, claiming that any faults in his translation belonged to the original.

Beardsley, himself fluent in French, then chipped in, complaining that Douglas's version was inadequate, and offering to make a fresh attempt, a proposal which outraged Bosie's hypersensitive pride. A furious tripartite row broke out between Wilde, Bosie and Beardsley, John Lane acting as reluctant arbitrator. When Oscar proposed to return Douglas's manuscript and do the job himself, Robbie Ross, although no admirer of Lord Alfred, pointed out that it would damage a promising literary career if Bosie's work were to be returned like a schoolboy's exercises, and *Salome* was eventually published in Wilde's own much-corrected version, with the peace-making dedication: 'To Lord Alfred Douglas, the translator of my play.'

Wilde was made physically ill by the imbroglio, and, to escape from Douglas, he took a fortnight's holiday, alone, in France. 'I required rest and freedom from the terrible strain of your companionship,' he was to recall. Douglas's flight into Egypt at the end of the year meant that on his return they only spent a few weeks together, and, his tormentor out of the way, Wilde embarked on his last prodigiously productive period of literary output. In the space of three months, he wrote *A Florentine Tragedy* and *La Sainte Courtisane*, destined for oblivion; *An Ideal Husband*, to be his next triumph; and had started on the scenario for his greatest play, *The Importance of Being Earnest*.

CHAPTER FOUR

Success and Failure

IMPOSSIBLE TO LIVE WITH, *nevertheless Bosie came to be considered by Wilde as increasingly central to his own creative life. Wilde persuaded himself that the destructive and self-destructive elements of Bosie's character could in some way be transformed into something finer. 'I thought life was going to be a brilliant comedy, and that you were to be one of many graceful figures in it,' he wrote in De Profundis. Convinced that life could be made to imitate art, Oscar willingly embraced the role of his own making in a drama destined to descend rapidly from high comedy into tragedy.*

During their long separation, however, Oscar was able to stand back and take a sober look at his relationship with Lord Alfred. Neither for the first nor the last time, he came to the conclusion that their

ABOVE: *Etching, by James Kelly, of Oscar Wilde with a child. 'It is absurd to talk of the ignorance of youth. The only people to whose opinions I listen are people much younger than myself.'*

LEFT: *Oscar photographed in New York by Napoleon Sarony during the famous session of 1882 which fixed Wilde's image in the imagination of his age.*

intimacy was ultimately destructive to him, and decided to break it off. But when Douglas returned from Cairo, he found he could not do without him, and they returned to their old pattern of life.

It was just after Bosie's return that Wilde and the Marquess of Queensberry first met. The Marquess saw the couple through the window at the Café Royal, and having poutingly accepted their invitation to join them, found to his surprise that Wilde was not the debauched Sporus his imagination had conjured up, but a charming and erudite gentleman. Oscar determined to use every ounce of his charm to make a good impression, and he regaled his guest with fables and stories, dwelling especially on the atheist themes he knew would amuse the Marquess. Their party continued until well past four, and Queensberry left them in the highest spirits. He retracted all the abuse he had formerly heaped upon Wilde, saying to Bosie, 'I don't wonder you are so fond of him; he is a wonderful man.'

By the time he got home, the Screaming Marquess, as Wilde always called him, had retracted his retraction. He wrote to his son that unless he broke off the intimacy with Wilde, he would be disowned

Contemporary photograph of the 'House Beautiful' at 16 Tite Street, from which Wilde had forcibly to eject the 'Screaming Scarlet Marquess' in 1894.

and disinherited. The letter was signed, 'Your disgusted so-called Father'. Bosie's reply was less than conciliatory. He sent a telegram stating simply: 'What a funny little man you are'. Their fight had now reached its climax, and both Douglases made sure that it was not allowed to cool.

Father and son hurled insults at each other by telegram and postcard, Bosie insisting that he would not, Queensberry insisting that he would give up the relationship. When the Marquess threatened that if he ever caught the two of them together he would thrash them, Bosie thoughtfully provided him with a complete itinerary of their movements. His bluff called, the Marquess, goaded by his son, stopped Bosie's meagre allowance, but, as Wilde later pointed out, this was no great hardship. He had always gone through through his yearly income in a few weeks, and privation in the noble cause of friendship gave him even greater cause to sponge off Oscar.

After Oscar and Bosie had been to Florence on a short holiday in May 1894, Queensberry decided to take action against the corrupter of his son. Having hired a burly pugilist to back him up, one night he turned up at Tite Street in person. As the two men were led into the library, Wilde politely rose to greet them, but the Marquess barked at him to 'sit down'.

Queensberry reeled off a string of libellous – but essentially true – allegations, to which Wilde asked, 'Do you seriously accuse your son and me of improper conduct?'

'I don't say you are it, but you look it, and you pose it, which is just as bad. If I catch you and my son together again in any public restaurant, I will thrash you,' Queensberry said.

'I don't know what the Queensberry rules are,' Wilde replied, 'but the Oscar Wilde rule is to shoot on sight. Leave my house at once.' The story goes that Wilde was obliged to manhandle the pugilist henchman out of the door, and gave instructions to his servant never to allow 'the most infamous brute in London' to enter his house again. It was this sort of incident that led Bosie to purchase the revolver that went off in a restaurant, causing another minor scandal.

That 'funny little man,' the Marquess of Queensberry, as seen by Max Beerbohm in 1894.

Wilde spent August to October 1894 with his family in Worthing, writing *The Importance of Being Earnest*. Bosie visited occasionally, but Oscar had decided to maintain a distance between them, and with Constance present, they could not indulge in their usual debauch. In October, however, *Earnest* completed, he agreed to spend his birthday in Brighton with Douglas.

There, Bosie came down with influenza. Oscar nursed him patiently through the fever, but as Douglas recovered, he fell ill himself. Far from repaying the kindnesses, Bosie simply left him to suffer in an inhospitable boarding house, and put his own renewed energies to sampling the pleasures of the

A.D. 1895.   No. 6907

16, Tite Street, Chelsea.

Catalogue of the Library of   *1 . 2 . 6*
                                 . 4 . 0
Valuable Books,   *P . 0*
                               . 18 . 0
Pictures, Portraits of Celebrities, Arundel Society Prints, *2 . 7 . 6*

HOUSEHOLD FURNITURE

CARLYLE'S WRITING TABLE,

Chippendale and Italian Chairs, Old Persian Carpets
and Rugs, Brass Fenders,

Moorish and Oriental Curiosities,

Embroideries, Silver and Plated Articles,

OLD BLUE AND WHITE CHINA,

Moorish Pottery, Handsome Ormolu Clock,
and numerous Effects –

The Property of Oscar Wilde,

Which will be Sold by Auction,

By Mr. BULLOCK,

ON THE PREMISES,

On Wednesday, April 24th, 1895,

AT ONE O'CLOCK.

May be Viewed the day prior, and Catalogues had of Messrs. CLARKE & Co.
16, Portugal Street, Lincoln's Inn; and of the Auctioneer,

211 HIGH HOLBORN, W.C,

town. When Wilde reproached him for this neglect, Bosie physically threatened him, and returned to London, leaving an abusive letter for Oscar to read, and astronomical bills for him to pay.

Finally Wilde seemed to realize that there was nothing good or pure left between them, and refused to answer any of the imploring telegrams Bosie sent, begging to be forgiven. All his good intentions came to nothing when, a few days later, Bosie's brother was discovered, lying dead in a ditch, a discharged shotgun by his side.

Lord Drumlanrig, Queensberry's eldest son and heir to the estates, was the most civilized, and least mad of the Douglas clan. Wilde had a great affection for him, calling him 'that candidissima anima', but his openness was no more defence against his father's extremes than Bosie's debauchery. As the Private Secretary to Lord Rosebery, then Foreign Secretary and possible Prime Minister, Drumlanrig had, with his father's approbation, accepted a peerage from his patron in the early 1890s. But when rumours reached the Marquess that his son and Rosebery were homosexually involved, he quarrelled with Drumlanrig, and followed Rosebery to the German spa town of Bad Homburg with a dog-whip, and was only restrained by the timely intervention of the Prince of Wales.

The death of Drumlanrig was recorded by the coroner as accidental, but it was widely believed to have been suicide, prompted by

Lord Alfred Douglas, the 'gilt-mailed boy' from Oxford, 'alone and palely loitering'. His hold over Wilde would never be broken.

homosexual blackmail. Queensberry had not spoken to his eldest son for over a year before the accident, and was quite distracted by the loss. His mental condition was exacerbated when, two days later, his second wife was granted a divorce on the grounds of his impotence, making him as unmanly as his sons.

Having lost two targets in two days, his quarrel with Bosie seemed now the only the only thing left to live for. His mood was fanned by the publication of a book, at first widely believed to have been written by Wilde himself, called *The Green Carnation*, which both satirised and glamorised the prevailing homosexuality of this fashionable clique. Although Oscar denied the attribution in the strongest terms – 'I invented that magnificent flower,' he wrote to the *Pall Mall Gazette*, 'but with the middle-class and mediocre book that usurps its strangely beautiful name I have nothing whatever to do' – he was secretly amused by the cleverness of its author, Robert Hichens, a journalist friend.

The Marquess of Queensberry was not the only threat to Wilde's ivory tower; for some time a gang of Alfred Taylor's boys had been blackmailing him. In a moment of casual and completely uncharacteristic generosity, Bosie had given a coat to one of them, but he had unfortunately neglected to search the pockets, in which he had left some of the love letters which Wilde had written to him.

Having sent various threats and demands, which Wilde only ignored, during rehearsals for *A Woman of No Importance* the blackmailers finally delivered a copy of one of Wilde's decorously suggestive notes, which was to become known as the 'Hyacinth' letter, to Herbert Beerbohm Tree. Tree passed it on to Wilde, commenting that it was 'open to misinterpretation', but Oscar jestingly explained that it was a poem in prose, and thus worthy of inclusion in the impeccably respectable Palgrave's *Golden Treasury*. When Tree objected that the note was not actually in verse, Wilde innocently replied 'that, no doubt, explains why it is not in the *Golden Treasury*'.

One night Wilde was approached at the stage door of the Haymarket Theatre by a William Allen, who offered to return the original of his letter for £10. 'You have no appreciation of literature,' was Wilde's suave response. 'If you had asked me for fifty, I might have given it to you. Besides, I already have a copy of that

Love and Death *by G.F. Watts. Death's foot 'is already on the threshold, while Love, a beautiful boy with lithe brown limbs is trying, with vain hands, to bar the entrance.'*

letter.' He was rattled, however, and in an attempt to bolster his claim for the literary value of the letter, he had Pierre Louÿs translate in into French.

The blackmailers would not give up so easily. One night Allen called at Tite Street with a soiled bundle containing all the Douglas letters, asking to be paid £30 for them. Wilde gave him a cheque for the money, but when he looked through the collection, the 'Hyacinth' letter was not among them. This omission was made good some days later, when Allen again called at Tite Street, this time, having heeded his victim's former advice, demanding £60. Out of patience, Wilde would have nothing to do with the blackmail, and gently sent him away.

Shortly after, yet another accomplice called on Wilde. 'I can't be bothered any more about that letter,' Oscar cried, 'I don't care tuppence about it.' To his surprise, the boy had been told to give the letter back: the gang had decided 'that there is no good trying to rent you, as you only laugh at us'. Wilde took the much-handled letter, and gave him ten shillings for a cab, adding archly, 'I am afraid that you are leading a wonderfully wicked life'.

An Ideal Husband opened in January 1894, and despite the muted tone of the critics over Wilde's previous work, they were now back on the offensive. George Bernard Shaw's review stands out both for its generosity and its perception. 'I am the only person in London who cannot sit down and write an Oscar Wilde play at will,' he wrote in the *Saturday Review*. Wilde, he wrote, 'has the property of making his critics dull. They laugh angrily at his epigrams, like a child who is coaxed into being amused in the very act of setting up a yell of rage and agony.'

Having seen that he had another hit on his hands, Wilde went with Bosie on holiday to Algiers,

Guido Reni's San Sebastiano, *the Saint whose name Wilde assumed during his exile. This painting and the preceding one by Watts were Wilde's favourite pictures.*

where they embarked on a concerted debauch. 'I have thoroughly demoralized this city,' he told the writer André Gide. A pleasant week was followed by a dreadful row, and Bosie ran off with a young boy to another resort, while Wilde returned via Paris to London. Everyone seemed to have presentiments of the impending disaster. Gide told him it would not be prudent to go back, but Oscar refused to listen: 'Prudent! How could I be that? I must go as far as possible. I cannot go any further. Something must happen… something else…'

The Importance of Being Earnest opened on St Valentine's Day 1895 at George Alexander's St James's Theatre, and, despite the violent snowstorm which was raging outside, the play had the warmest possible reception. One actor recalled that 'in my fifty-three years of acting, I never remember a greater triumph'. Wilde himself was slightly disconcerted by his play's almost unchallenged success. 'There are two ways of disliking my plays,' he would later remark, 'one is to dislike them, the other is to prefer Earnest.'

Charles Ricketts, who painted the real Portrait of Mr. W. H., *which was stolen from Tite Street during the auction of Wilde's effects in 1895.*

The Marquess of Queensberry had booked a ticket for the performance, but the management noticed the fact, and, sensing trouble, cancelled his reservation. In order to prevent any disturbance, they also took the wise precaution of placing policemen at the entrances. Wilde himself, lest the Marquess managed slip in via the stage door disguised as a policeman, spent the performance backstage. When the ticketless Queensberry did arrive, carrying a 'phallic bouquet' of carrots and turnips to hurl at Oscar, he was turned away.

Still smarting from the successful rebuff, three days later he marched into the Albemarle, Wilde's club, and left on the mantelpiece his card, on which he had written the lines that were to be Wilde's ruin. 'To Oscar Wilde, posing Somdomite,' read his famously illegible

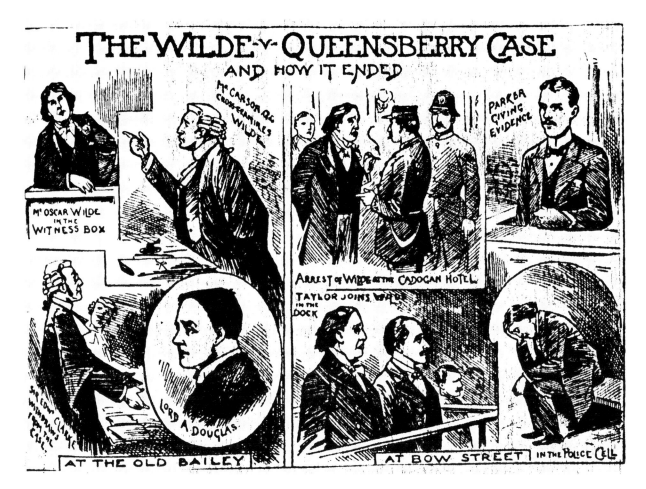

'Industry and Idleness.' Edward Carson and
Oscar Wilde, who attended Trinity College
together, meeting again at the Old Bailey in 1895.
The trial was a sensation. This and the following
cartoons are from The Police News.

and illiterate scrawl. The porter immediately removed the card and discreetly placed it in an envelope to await the poet's return. Would that Oscar had observed his discretion.

Meanwhile, Oscar had gone to the country for a post-first-night victory tour of grand country houses. On his return on 28 February, his first call was to Ricketts and Shannon, but their meeting for some reason lacked the usual gaiety of such occasions. Having unsuccessfully tried to persuade them to publish his ingenious cod-Shakesperian essay 'The Portrait of Mr. W. H.', which had previously inspired Ricketts to execute a brilliant pastiche portrait, in melancholy mood he left them for the West End. He called at the Albemarle, and the porter handed him the sealed envelope containing the Marquess's card.

THE ILLUSTRATED Police News

LAW COURTS AND WEEKLY RECORD ~

ESTABLISHED 1864.

No. 1628. [REGISTERED FOR CIRCULATION IN THE UNITED KINGDOM AND ABROAD.] SATURDAY, MAY 4, 1895. Price One Penny

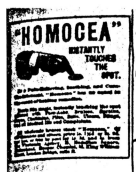

CLOSING SCENE AT THE OLD BAILEY.

TRIAL OF OSCAR WILDE

OSCAR WILDE AS A LECTURER 1882 AMERICA.

OSCAR WILDE AS A PRISONER 1895 BOW STREET

JURY

SALE OF OSCAR WILDE'S EFFECTS

OSCAR WILDE'S HOUSE IN TITE STREET.

Deeply shocked by its contents, Wilde went immediately to his hotel on Piccadilly, from where he summoned Robbie Ross to advise him. 'My whole life seems ruined by this man,' he wrote. 'The Tower of Ivory is assailed by the foul thing. On the sand is my life spilt.' Ross confirmed Wilde's own opinion that the only way to be rid of the Screaming Marquess was to have him locked up, and the next morning both men went to see Ross's solicitor, Charles Humphreys.

Having obtained Wilde's assurance of his total innocence of the slur, Humphreys advised that a libel case against the Marquess of Queensberry would certainly be victorious. They obtained a warrant for his apprehension, and on 2 March, Queensberry was arrested and charged with criminal libel. The train of events that was to lead to such tragedy had been put into unstoppable motion.

At his arraignment on the 9 March, it became apparent that the Marquess had, beyond supposition,

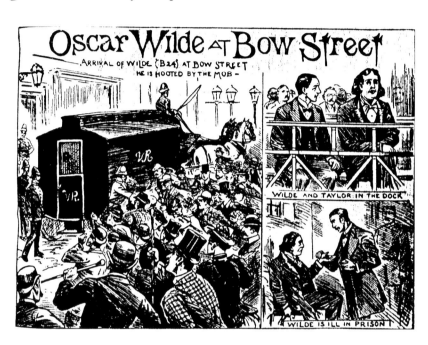

The end of the First Act of Wilde's legal drama. Wilde experiences the less adulatory attention of the London mob as he is taken to Bow Street after Queensberry's acquittal.

common gossip, Wilde's own writings, and a few of Wilde's letters, precious little evidence to back up his allegation. Feeling confident, Wilde and Bosie set off on a jaunt to Monte Carlo, but, advised by his own lawyers that the penalty for a criminal libel was two years imprisonment, and that on the scanty evidence he had presented to the magistrate's court he was in grave danger of enjoying Her Majesty's Pleasure, Queensberry began in earnest to search for more incriminating evidence against Wilde. He and his agents had found nothing, until by chance they approached an actor who had taken a minor role in *An Ideal Husband*. Charles Brookfield had nursed a dislike for Wilde since they had met during the American tour, and his enmity had been fanned by Wilde's contemptuous treatment of an æsthetic burlesque Brookfield had once written.

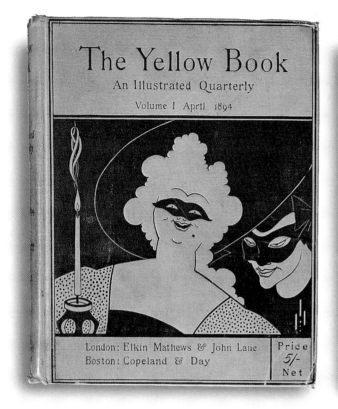

The Yellow Book, *the artistic magazine,*
was nearly destroyed because Wilde was
said to have had 'a book with a yellow
cover' with him on his arrest at the
Cadogan Hotel.

By a mixture of personal experience and theatrical gossip, Brookfield was able to direct Queensberry's detectives to a prostitute willing to state that 'her profession had suffered from Wilde's activities'; more damagingly, he gave them the name and address of Alfred Taylor. The detectives broke into Taylor's apartments, discovered his address book, and finally had access to the gang that had been blackmailing Wilde. By means of threats, coercion and bribery, Queensberry suborned enough witnesses to transform his case.

On Wilde's return, he found his forthcoming case was the talk of London. The Douglas clan – Bosie, his remaining brother Percy and Lady Queensberry – rallied behind Oscar, hailing him as their champion, and offering to pay all his costs, while his own more prudent friends strongly advised him to drop the suit and leave immediately for the Continent. 'Everyone wants me to go abroad,' Oscar told Frank Harris. 'I have just been abroad, and now I have come home again. One can't keep going abroad unless one is a missionary, or, what comes to the same thing, a commercial traveller.'

The transcripts of Oscar Wilde's trials, as compiled with such admirable forensic skill by H. Montgomery Hyde, make compelling, if depressing reading. They are the only account of the trial in which we can see, complete and untainted by prejudices, the power of Oscar's brilliant intellect. On the first day, 3 April, 1895, he ran circles round Edward Carson, Queensberry's QC, with whom he had been at Trinity College. He treated Carson's serious questions with levity, his attempts at levity with derision, and Wilde left the court believing that he would win the case, saying to one friend, 'All is well. The working classes are with me … to a boy.'

On the second day, however, matters did not go so well. Oscar was over-confident, and Carson was determined to revenge himself for his mauling the day before. He laid subtle traps that Wilde naïvely fell into time and again, and, by the end of the day, all Oscar's high spirits had disappeared. When, on the third and final day it became clear that Carson was about to produce a clutch of Alfred Taylor's boys, Wilde's lawyer, Sir Edward Clarke, advised his client that he had no choice but to withdraw from the suit, and the jury was ordered by the judge to return a 'not guilty' verdict. The afternoon editions of the newspapers placarded the result in their boldest type. Jerome K. Jerome, the popular novelist, went so far as to demand the 'heads of the five hundred noblemen and men-of-the world who share his turpitude and corrupt youth', a call that reveals more a self-righteous indignation than a knowledge of the London homosexual underworld.

By withdrawing, Wilde now lay open to a prosecution on charges that he had, effectively, admitted. A warrant for his arrest was immediately sought, but not granted for several hours, to give him time to escape to France. But Oscar did not, as was widely expected he would, take a place on the early evening boat train that left Victoria Station every day for the Continent; even so, its carriages were filled by scores of well-dressed but worried-looking gentlemen with hastily-packed bags. Instead, Oscar went to lunch near the Old Bailey with Bosie and Robbie Ross. Having written to the *Evening News* to explain his actions, he went with Robbie to the Cadogan Hotel, where he

The Cadogan Hotel, Sloane Street, where Robbie Ross and Oscar Wilde, drinking hock and seltzer, awaited the inevitable deus ex machina *of the drama.*

remained, drinking hock and seltzer, until the arrival at half past six of two police officers. 'Mr Wilde, I believe?' they inquired. 'Yes, yes,' he said, and as they led him away, 'a yellow book under his arm', it was noticed that, perhaps for the first time in his life, he was visibly drunk.

A carriage took Oscar to Bow Street Police Court, where he was charged, and there he spent the first of many nights in custody. Extraordinarily, journalists were allowed into the cells to view the shamed prisoner through the bars, and in the morning, when bail was quite improperly refused, Wilde was taken to Holloway Prison, there to remain until his case came up.

Public indignation at Wilde and 'his sort' reached a crescendo. References in the press to the 'yellow book under his arm' (in fact it was a copy of *Aphrodite*, a slightly erotic book by Wilde's Paris friend Pierre Louÿs) led members of the public to stone the windows of John Lane's offices where *The Yellow Book*, that symbol of nineties' decadence, was published. Ironically, Oscar had always been disdainful of this publication, and had never contributed to its supposedly lurid pages. Lane, touring America at the time, panicked, and agreed to dismiss Aubrey Beardsley from his post as Art Editor in order to appease the moral indignation of his public, and several of his authors. The scandal, he recalled years later, 'killed *The Yellow Book*, and it almost killed me'.

On his return to London, Lane took further steps to distance himself and the Bodley Head (or Sodley Bed, as it was quipped at the time) from the influence of Wilde and his *côterie*. Having sacked Beardsley, he returned the manuscript of *The Duchess of Padua*, and withdrew all Wilde's books from circulation, Henceforth, Wilde and Beardsley would be in the same boat, bereft of their incomes, and in search of a new, less pusillanimous publisher, a role which Leonard Smithers, art dealer, publisher and pornographer, would play with some aplomb.

Wilde's arrest had another and yet more disastrous consequence: immediately, all his creditors – tradesmen and moneylenders, hoteliers and restaurateurs – had hurried over to Tite Street to try to recover what they were owed. Although the creditors had been prepared to wait, the monies that Douglas and Lady Queensberry had promised Oscar did not materialise, and, with Wilde's damages and costs pending, Queensberry maliciously forced a sale of Wilde's possessions. Much was stolen by souvenir hunters during the viewing period before the auction, and Oscar's precious library, including all the exquisite editions and presentation copies of the books of the last twenty years, all his china, his pictures and other treasures were knocked down at bargain prices. Though it was said that every house-maid in Chelsea could be seen walking away from the house with some souvenir of the monster, the sale still did not raise enough money.

An Englishman's idea of support was once memorably defined as giving a man an umbrella when the sun shines, and demanding it back when it rains. Incarcerated, and now penniless, Wilde was also deserted by the friends in society whom he had amused for so long. Only a few brave souls, most of them artists or writers, were prepared to stick by him.

In a gesture of generosity both men were to regret, Sir Edward Clarke, continuing to believe Wilde's assurances of his innocence, offered to represent him without charge. The day before Oscar's trial, Bosie left London for the Continent, persuaded by Clarke that even his presence in London would count against Wilde. To his credit, he had refused to go until specifically instructed to do so by Oscar, and Robbie Ross followed him soon after.

In the light of the evidence Carson had been about to produce at the Queensberry trial, Alfred Taylor had also been arrested; refusing to turn informer, he, too, had been charged. The two men were brought before the Old Bailey on 26 April. Clarke attempted to separate their trials, on the grounds that to try them together would be prejudicial to Wilde, but the request was rejected, and thus Taylor's noble action in keeping silence became a mixed blessing to Wilde, as his own defence was tainted through being associated with that of the procurer.

All the evidence that Queensberry had so carefully amassed was given to the prosecution, and though much of it was rightly dismissed by the judge as being tainted by perjury, misrepresentation and purchase, more than enough remained to form a solid prosecution case. Oscar behaved with impressive dignity as the propriety of his poems, of *Dorian Gray*, of his letters to Bosie and others were raked over again, and the trial of both men ended with a hung jury, at least one, and possibly as many as three refusing to convict in the face of the perjured evidence. In the normal course of events, Wilde would probably have been released at this stage, but such was the general feeling against him, such was society's delight that the jester was in its power, that a second trial was immediately ordered.

Released on bail, Oscar went to the Midland Hotel at King's Cross, where rooms had been reserved for him. He had not been there long when he was asked to leave. The Marquess of Queensberry had sent his henchmen to intimidate the manager, and Oscar was forced back on to the street. The same process was repeated in hotel after hotel, until finally Wilde shook off his pursuers, and at midnight his cab pulled up at the house in Oakley Street where Lady Wilde and his brother were living. 'Give me shelter, Willie,' he begged, before collapsing 'like a wounded stag', 'let me lie on the floor or I shall die on the streets.'

Wilde was again urged by his friends to flee England. Frank Harris always claimed that he had placed at Wilde's disposal a steam yacht moored at Erith: 'She has steam up now,' he told him, 'one hundred pounds pressure to the square inch in her boilers, her captain's waiting, her crew ready. If one started now, one could breakfast at Boulogne.' But Wilde would not consider flight. 'I can't. I dare not,' he told Harris. 'I'm caught in a trap. I can only wait for the end. I could not go about France feeling that the policeman's hand might fall on my shoulder at any moment. I could not live a life of fear and doubt. It would kill me in a month.'

Neither would Speranza, optimistic at having survived two trials herself, let him go: 'If you stay, even if you go to prison, you will always be my son; it will make no difference to my affection. But if you leave, I will never speak to you again.' Willie, too, offered his own almost endearing form of support, telling everyone who asked, 'Oscar is an Irish gentleman. He will stay and face the music.' He was in the habit of adding, 'Oscar is not a man of bad character. You could trust him with a woman anywhere,' and when W.B. Yeats called with letters of support, Oscar told him of Willie's ridiculous defence, adding, 'My poor dear brother, he could compromise a steam engine.'

Bosie and Ross, now in France, could not visit him; Sherard, who had been in Paris trying to raise money from Sarah Bernhardt, found him in a dull, dark room surrounded by dying flowers. 'Why have you brought me no poison from Paris,' asked Wilde. His dear and loyal friend Ada Leverson, 'the Sphinx', found him fearfully depressed by his surroundings, and offered shelter at her grand house in South Kensington. There, to avoid compromising his hosts, Oscar remained in the nursery during the day, only coming down for dinner. While at Courtfield Gardens he was visited by his wife Constance, who implored him to leave the country before the next trial. He refused even her.

His second trial lasted four days. The prosecution, led by the Solicitor General himself, was well rehearsed and had pruned itself of Queensberry's unreliable and dishonest witnesses. Wilde had sat for a portrait by the legendary drinker Toulouse-Lautrec the night before, and was tired and haggard: his performance for once lacked lustre in the repetition. The defence won a minor victory when the judge agreed to separate Wilde's and Taylor's cases, but when Taylor was speedily convicted, thereby helping to damn Wilde, any hope of a victory must have departed. After Taylor's verdict, Queensberry, on his way to celebrate, met his son Percy in the street. The two exchanged blows, and had to be separated by a policeman. Undaunted, they merely walked around the corner and set upon each other again, and were eventually bound over to keep the peace.

In Wilde's trial, the jury returned guilty verdicts on all counts but one. The judge sentenced him to be imprisoned and kept to hard labour for two years, 'the severest sentence that the law allows'. 'In my judgement,' he added for good measure, 'it is totally inadequate for such a case as this.' W.B. Yeats, who watched Wilde being led away from the court in chains, watched harlots in the street dancing in celebration: one was heard to call out, ''E'll 'ave 'is 'air cut reg'lar now!'

TOP LEFT: *Edward Carson, prosecuted. In the first trial Oscar ran rings around him.*

ABOVE: *Sir Alfred Wills, Mr Justice Wills, presiding judge: 'It is the worst case I have ever tried.'*

LEFT: *Sir Edward Clarke represented Oscar for no charge, a gesture both men were to regret.*

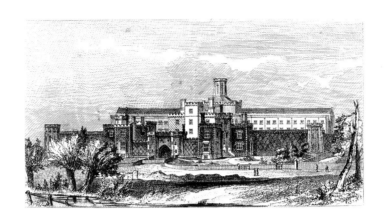

CHAPTER FIVE

De Profundis

DISCIPLINE AND REGULARITY *were the keywords of life at Pentonville, Wandsworth and Reading Prisons, where Oscar was to pass the next two years. When not working or eating, prisoners were kept to their cells and were known only by the numbers on the doors; like animals they were worked hard, and fed and watered at regular times. No one was actually 'reformed', they were not there for that purpose: they were there to be punished. To follow Wilde through the penal system seems almost an indiscretion, as the proud, immaculately groomed, and once almost respectable gentleman degenerated under its oppressive regime. But like Byron's Prisoner of Chillon, Oscar's greatest punishment was to be shut away from the world, ignored and forgotten.*

LEFT: The Exercise Yard *by Vincent van Gogh. 'With slouch and swing around the ring/ We trod the Fools' Parade!/And shaven head and feet of lead/Make a merry masquerade.'*

From the Old Bailey, he was driven to Newgate, and two days later to Pentonville Prison. Regulations stated that prisoners were allowed no books but the Bible, the Book of Common Prayer and a hymnal; one visitor was permitted every three months, and during that time one letter could be sent and received. Private influence still pertained to a small degree though, and through the Home Secretary, Herbert Asquith, it was arranged for a few books to be brought in to Wilde. Wilde waggishly suggested he should be sent Flaubert's *Madame Bovary*, but in a penitential state of mind he revised this to the works of Saint Augustine.

A less welcome privilege came in the form of a visit from Queensberry's solicitors, who brought demands for full payment of the Marquess's legal fees in the libel trial. Unable to meet their demands, Wilde enjoyed a brief moment of humiliating freedom at the bankruptcy court, but the sight of 'Little Robbie' Ross, in full view of the open court, gravely raising his hat in silent and solemn salute to his friend, was to be a fathomless source of solace to Oscar in the darkest moments of his life in prison.

Under the insanitary conditions and brutalising regime Wilde fell seriously ill, and one morning found himself unable to get out of his plank bed. Threatened with the most draconian punishments for malingering, he managed to raise himself, but fainted at chapel, badly injuring his ear, and was taken to the prison infirmary. Representations were made to the government to the effect that Pentonville prison was about to kill its most illustrious prisoner, but the doctors despatched to assess his condition found him sitting on his bed, laughing and regaling his fellows with tales, just as though he was back in the Café Royal.

In spite of his apparent good health, the injury to his ear, from which he never properly recovered, led the doctors to recommend that Wilde be moved to the country, and Oscar was transferred by train to Reading Prison late in 1895. The journey would have been unpleasant enough for a man accustomed to the relative

INTERIOR VIEW OF THE PRISON PALACE AT READING.

Reading Gaol, where the kindnesses of Major Nelson and Warder Martin mitigated the worst of Oscar's suffering.

Entrance to the Exposition Universelle, *1889 by
Jean Beraud. At the Musée D'Orsay, Wilde's voice
is said to have been captured by the Edison
Phonograph, reciting excerpts from* The Ballad of
Reading Gaol.

luxuries of first-class travel, but a worse humiliation was to come: 'From two o'clock till half-past two that day I had to stand on the centre platform at Clapham Junction in convict dress and handcuffed, for the world to look at. I had been taken out of the Hospital Ward without a moment's notice being given to me. Of all possible objects I was the most grotesque. When people saw me they laughed. Each train as it came up swelled the audience. Nothing could exceed their amusement. That was of course before they knew who I was. As soon as they had been informed, they laughed still more. For half an hour I stood there in the grey November rain surrounded by a jeering mob.'

Various attempts were made, by Frank Harris, by Robbie Ross and George Bernard Shaw, during the course of Wilde's imprisonment, to have his sentence mitigated, but as Hesketh Pearson puts it in his magnificent and unsurpassed 1946 biography, 'although Wilde had harmed no one but himself, not a single prominent man in any country could be persuaded to save him a day's torture by signing a piece of paper', and their petitions came to nothing.

The regime at Reading was, to begin with, little easier than that at Pentonville; if the air was less fetid, the food was no better, the beds no softer. Oscar was relieved of the back-breaking work of picking oakum, and transferred to work in the garden and the prison library. His self-respect, on the brink of annihilation, was given a much-needed boost when Robert Sherard arranged for a production in Paris of *Salome* in March 1896. That, he later wrote 'was the thing that turned the scales in my favour', the moment that the authorities realised that they had not managed to destroy him.

The chaplains and doctors were narrow-minded prigs who patronised and insulted their illustrious prisoner. 'Mr Wilde,' asked one, 'did you have morning prayers in your house?' 'I fear not,' he replied. 'You see where you are now.' But humanity showed itself in the unexpected kindness of a few of the warders, who behaved with uncalled-for courtesy. Wilde was soon helping them to enter newspaper competitions, once even winning a grand piano. He formed an especially good relationship with one Thomas Martin, who brought him newspapers and decent food, and in return Oscar attempted in a haphazard and, one suspects, ultimately misleading way, to complete his education.

Meanwhile, Wilde wrote nothing to Douglas, and Douglas in his turn wrote nothing to him. Informed that Bosie was about to include some of his letters in a French newspaper article, Wilde was deeply hurt that his permission had not been sought; when he discovered he was to receive the dedication of Douglas's new volume of poems, he refused, through Ross, the dubious honour, and for good measure demanded the return of all his letters, and all the jewellery he had given Douglas. He justifiably felt that while he languished in a prison cell, Lord Alfred was capitalising on his dreadful plight.

※ ※ ※

On 3 February 1896, Lady Wilde died after a long and painful illness. Rather than have him hear the news from a stranger, Constance, who was also very ill and would not survive her husband, travelled from Switzerland to tell him herself. Immediately after his conviction, she had started proceedings for divorce, but when he begged her not to take the step, she concurred, although she did change her and the children's names to Holland.

In the middle of that year, a new governor was sent to administer Reading, and the installation of Major Nelson marked a sea change for Wilde. Suddenly, he was allowed to keep a limited library, and

*Wilde's bill, under the name Sebastian Melmoth, at
Dupoirier's Hôtel d'Alsace. 'I am dying beyond my
means,' he told Ross. 'I will never outlive the century.
The English people would not stand for it.'*

the publisher Arthur Humphreys sent him over fifty books on various subjects. His health started to improve rapidly. Still forbidden to write anything but his quarterly letter, Oscar hit upon the idea of writing an extended epistle to Alfred Douglas, and Nelson agreed that this – though stretching the point – was within the rules, and allowed him pens, paper, and, most wonderfully, a light. Provisionally entitled *Epistola: In Carcere et Vinculis*, the work which Robbie Ross was later to publish as *De Profundis* was intended to draw a line under Wilde's relationship with Bosie.

     Full of profound and poetic moments, his attempt at writing a personal testament in the manner of Saints Augustine or Theresa has been described as Wilde's greatest work of fiction. And in spite of its

faults, *De Profundis* is a deeply moving document. If its prose is a little purple here and there, we must remember the circumstances under which it was written; if its structure is slightly clumsy in places, we should be amazed that the entire piece was written in a single draft, and that Wilde never revised the work.

At last, after two years, the nightmare ended. To spare him the gauntlet of a curious press, Major Nelson had Wilde secretly transferred to Pentonville the night before his release. More Adey and Stewart Headlam, two of Wilde's faithful friends, met him at the gates of the prison at dawn the next morning, 19 May 1897. From there, they drove to Headlam's house, which he entered 'with the dignity of a king returning from exile', recalled Ada Leverson, 'talking, laughing, smoking a cigarette. He looked markedly better, slighter, and younger than he had two years previously.' 'Sphinx,' he greeted her warmly, on his entrance, 'how marvellous of you to know exactly the right hat to wear at seven o'clock in the morning to meet a friend who has been away.'

Almost immediately, having embraced the friends and acquaintances who called to see him, he left with Adey for Newhaven, and the boat to France. He would never return to England again. Robbie Ross and Reggie Turner were waiting to meet him and his few possessions at four the next morning in Dieppe. As all of Oscar's belongings had been either sold or looted from the house in Tite Street, a wardrobe of clothes had been assembled for him, together with a dressing-case marked with the initials S. M. They stood for Sebastian Melmoth, the alias he was to use from now on until his death. His new name was carefully chosen. Sebastian was for the martyred Saint, and Melmoth for the Wanderer from the gothic novel by Charles Maturin, from whom his mother was descended.

At Dieppe, he checked into the Hôtel Sandwich, and was almost back to his old sparkling form.

The Hôtel d'Alsace, on Paris's Left Bank, where Wilde spent his last months. 'My wallpaper and I are fighting a duel to the death. One or the other of us has to go.'

LEFT: *Wilde in Rome after his release. On this visit he received seven Blessings from the Pope: 'my walking stick showed signs of budding,' he joked.*

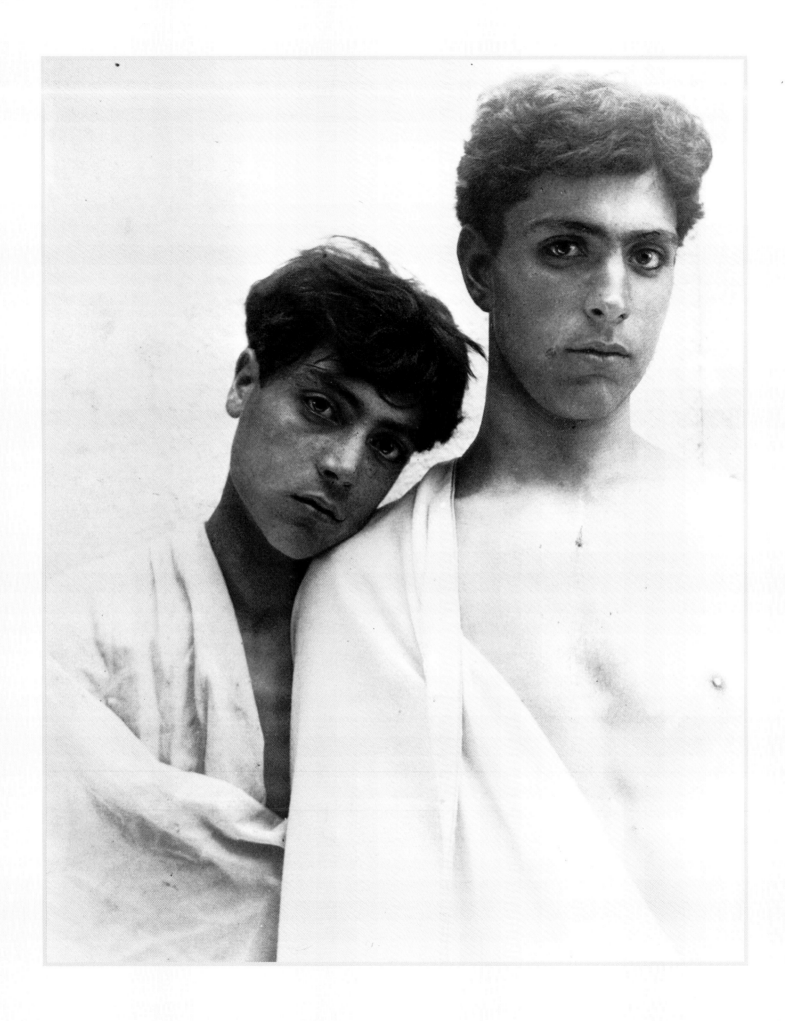

'I have thought it better that Robbie should stay here under the name of Reginald Turner,' he quipped, 'and Reggie under the name of R. B. Ross. It is better that they should not use their own names.'

The last phase of his life, the years of exile – perhaps the most devastating and heartbreaking of all the states of the soul – had begun.

Wilde was not broken by his time in prison. He had told his friend, Warder Martin, 'I never intend to laugh, nor do I intend ever again to write anything calculated to produce laughter in others. I have vowed to dedicate my life to Tragedy. If I write any more books, it will be to form a library of lamentations. They will be written in a style begotten of sorrow, in sentences composed in solitude, and punctuated by tears. I shall be an enigma to the world of Pleasure, but a mouthpiece for the world of Pain.' The vow was made not in defeat, but because Oscar had fathomed the bottomless malice of the world, and determined never again to pander to it.

Two days before his release, Wilde had begged his friend and benefactor Martin to give a biscuit to a frightened child, imprisoned for its inability to pay a paltry fine. Martin had agreed, but his kindness was discovered and he was dismissed for this petty breach of prison rules. One of Wilde's first actions after his release was to write a long and impassioned attack on the brutality of the British penal system, published in the *Daily Chronicle* on 28 May under the title 'The Case of Warder Martin'.

His next, and as it would turn out, last, literary effort was an attempt to be faithful to his promise to search for pathos. *The Ballad of Reading Gaol* was written during the summer of 1897, and published early the next year by Leonard Smithers, 'the most learned pornographer in Europe'. He was the only London publisher whom Wilde was prepared to trust, since Wilde could be sure that the erotomane who loved nothing more than to bate the authorities with signs in his shop window announcing 'Smut is cheap today' would always act with a total absence of prurience.

On Wilde's release, an American newspaper had offered him a large sum to write a memoir of his time in prison. Oscar replied that he could not understand how such an offer could be made to a gentleman. Fernaud Xau, editor of Paris's *Le Journal*, offered him a position at the head of his list of contributors, but, as Sherard reports, he courteously declined the proposition. 'Some people might read what I choose to write out of morbidness, but I don't want that; I wish to be read for Art's sake, not for my notoriety.' And thus he committed himself to squandering his vast talents on conversation, not art.

The author of *Reading Gaol* was announced on the title page as only C. 3. 3., which had been the number of Wilde's cell at Reading. Although C. 3. 3.'s identity could hardly have been a secret, the public mood in England had changed during Wilde's incarceration to sympathy for the poet, and for

LEFT: *Fisher boys of Taormina. On a trip Oscar met Baron von Gloeden who photographed naked boys and sold the pictures.*

once, Oscar was not excoriated by his critics. 'The whole,' wrote one, 'is as awful as the pages of Sophocles. That he has rendered, with his fine art, so much of the essence of his life, and the life of others in that inferno to the sensitive, is a memorable thing for literature. This is a simple, a poignant, a great ballad, one of the greatest in the English language.'

The book sold well, and Smithers, more at home with the printing of tiny private editions, found it difficult to keep up with the demand for fresh impressions. Wilde wryly observed that, 'Leonard is so fond of suppressed books that he even suppresses his own.'

Oscar made attempts to reconcile himself to his wife, who, by her journey to inform him of Speranza's death, had shown how much she still loved him. On his release she agreed to pay him an allowance, and agreed that, after a year, provided that he did not see Lord Alfred, a reunion with his wife and children could be arranged. The prospect of a lonely winter in France, however, led him to beg that his probation be cut short. Her curt reply, influenced by everyone's desire to keep Wilde and Bosie apart, incensed and insulted him, and he immediately arranged a meeting with Douglas. Despite the cruelties expressed in *De Profundis*, and Bosie's proven callousness, their friendship reignited, and they agreed to take a trip to Italy together.

It was a disaster, as Oscar told Ross: 'Bosie, for four months, by endless letters, offered me a home. He offered me love, affection, and care, and promised that I should never want for anything. But when we met on our way to Naples, I found that he had no money, no plans, and had forgotten all his promises. When my allowance ceased, he left.' With Bosie's departure, any chance of Oscar's ever leading a contented life was destroyed, for Constance was no longer prepared to see him; she died at Genoa in April 1898, and he never saw his children again.

Bosie had once defended the profligacy in which he indulged at Oscar's expense: 'I had nothing to contribute. Everything that I had and was going to have in the future was and always will be his.' When his father died in January 1900, Douglas did not live up to his those words, and refused to give Wilde anything but pittances. When he complained of such treatment, Lord Alfred accused Oscar of behaving 'like an old whore'.

Having spent the first months of his freedom on the Brittany coast, followed by another few months with and without Bosie in Naples, Wilde moved to Paris in 1898, and rarely left it again. Those respectable Englishmen who came to France were careful to cut him, and he had expected, even looked

RIGHT: *Taormina in Sicily to where Oscar was reputed to have travelled from Naples in December 1897.*

forward to such treatment: 'To be spoken about, and not spoken to, is delightful,' he had once said. But when former friends like George Alexander gratuitously snubbed him, he was deeply hurt. Alexander later made up for the slight by giving Wilde royalties on *Lady Windermere's Fan* and *Earnest*, the rights to which he had bought during Wilde's bankruptcy proceedings.

By stages, Wilde became a tragic figure. Money came in sporadically, and was spent with the same lack of concern as ever. Some friends simply gave it to him, while others, more delicate, bought options on future literary works which all parties knew would never materialise. Looking shabby, his former pride in his dress and toilette gone for ever, Oscar slipped into the habit of importuning old friends, and even perfect strangers; even his sole remaining asset, his talk, became worn and threadbare, and like Brummell before him, he cut a sorry figure.

He had the same old trouble with hotel bills, and the quality of his apartments slipped further and further towards the lowest class of accommodation. Having had to be rescued from serious pecuniary embarrassment at another hotel by M. Dupoirier, proprietor of the Hôtel d'Alsace, in August 1899, he stayed at the Alsace, apart from one or two trips abroad, right until the very end.

His death crept slowly upon him. The injury to his ear had never been repaired, and late in October, 1900, he was told that an operation on the ear was essential. Unable to afford it, had to borrow the money. 'I fear I shall die beyond my means,' he joked.

The operation was not successful, and led swiftly to cerebral meningitis. For the last weeks of his life Oscar was in excruciating pain, often delirious and, while not frightened by death, terrified of dying alone. He would not, at least, be allowed to suffer that final humiliation.

On the morning of 29 November, 1900, with Wilde now at death's door, Robbie Ross, recalling that long ago his friend had reflected that 'Catholicism is the only religion to die in' and remembering his own promise to 'bring a priest when Oscar was no longer in a fit condition to shock one', called for a priest. Wilde was unable to speak when the man arrived, but he was able to indicate that he indeed did wish to be received into the Church he had long been tempted by. Twenty-four hours later, cradled in the arms of the devoted and faithful hotelier Dupoirier, at the age of just forty-seven, Oscar Wilde was pronounced dead.

IL Y A TRENTE ANS

Oscar Wilde mourait dans mes bras

...nous dit M. Dupoirier, ancien propriétaire de l'Hôtel d'Alsace

— Un soir, on vint me dire : « Il y a, à l'hôtel du 4 de la rue des Beaux-Arts, un locataire qui veut loger désormais chez vous. Il faut aller chercher ses affaires ». Je me rendis chez ce monsieur. Il me dit s'appeler Sébastien Melmotte. C'était un grand type d'Anglais large et gros en proportion. Il pesait bien 100 kilos.

Je pris les deux valises dont l'une en cuir jaune, que je possède encore, marquée aux initiales S. M., la canne, le parapluie, et je portais le tout au troisième étage de l'hôtel d'Alsace que je tenais avec ma femme.

Ainsi me parle M. Dupoirier, qui eut l'honneur d'héberger pendant

M. Dupoirier's recollections of the last hours of Oscar Wilde, who died in his arms and in his debt; they were published in a Paris newspaper in 1930.

Wilde's death was a merciful release from a life that had become insupportable. His end was curiously symbolic of the closing of the 1890s, and the beginning of a century of barbarous Philistinism, and what it lacked in nobility, it more than made up for in pathos. He wrote his epitaph himself.

'I was a man who stood in symbolic relations to the art and culture of my age. I had realized this for myself at the very dawn of my manhood, and had forced my age to realize it afterwards. Few men hold such a position in their lifetime and have it so acknowledged. It is usually discerned, if it is discerned at all, by the historian, or the critic, long after both the man and his age have passed away. With me it was different. I felt it myself, and made others feel it.

'I made art a philosophy, and philosophy an art: I altered the minds of men, and the colour of things: I awoke the imagination of my century so that it created myth and legend around me: I summed up all things in a phrase, all existence in an epigram: whatever I touched I made beautiful.'

And alien tears will fill for him

Pity's long-broken urn,

For his mourners will be outcast men,

And outcasts always mourn.

RIGHT: *Oscar Wilde's tomb at Père Lachaise cemetery. 'Ah, Robbie, when we are dead and buried in our porphyry tombs, and the trumpet of the Last Judgement is sounded, I shall turn and whisper to you, "Robbie, Robbie, let us pretend we do not hear it."'*

ABOVE: *Blue plaque unveiled by Sir Compton McKenzie at Oscar Wilde's Tite Street house in 1954. H. Montgomery Hyde and the Mayor of Chelsea look on.*

OSCAR WILDE

The stained glass window at Westminster Abbey,
finally installed in 1995 in Oscar Wilde's memory.

Index

ACKNOWLEDGEMENTS

ABBREVIATIONS:

Bord Failte / Irish Tourist Board - BF
Bridgeman Art Library - BAL
Corbis - Bettmann - CB
Hulton Getty Picture Collection - HG
Victoria & Albert Museum / Enthoven Collection - VA
Collection Viollet - CV
Weidenfeld & Nicolson Archive - WN

Endpapers. BAL / The Design Library, New York
page 2. CB
page 3. HG
page 7. CB
page 9. HG
page 10. HG
page 11. WN
page 12. CV
page 13. BF
page 14. Above Courtesy Board Trinity College, Dublin
page 14. Below BF
page 15. HG
page 16. HG
page 17. BAL/John Bethell
page 18. BAL / Giraudon (Musee des Beaux-Arts, Nantes)
page 20. WN
page 21. WN
page 22. HG
page 23. HG

page 25. Barnaby's Picture Library / Fotomas Index
page 27. VA
page 28. VA
page 30. BAL / Private Collection
page 31. Ashmolean Museum, Oxford (courtesy Eva Reichmann)
page 32. CB
page 34. BAL / Private Collection
page 35. HG
page 36. BAL / Brooklyn Museum, New York
page 38. above left BAL (Chateau de Versailles)
page 38. above right BAL (Musee des Beaux Arts, Rouen-Giraudon) *
page 38. below BAL (Musee d'Orsay, Paris)
page 39. above BAL (Musee des Beaux Arts,

Rouen-Giraudon).*
page 39. below left (Musee d'Orsay, Paris)
page 39. below right (Musee d'Orsay, Paris-Lauros, Giraudon)
page 41. CB
page 42. CV
page 45. BAL / A Pope Family Trust
page 46. HG
page 47. Freer Gallery, Smithsonian Institution, Washington
page 50. above WN
page 50-51. Camera Press
page 53. WN
page 56. Interlink Productions New York / photo Nick Wood
page 58. above left HG.*
page 58-59. WN
page 61. WN
page 62. HG

page 65. WN
page 66-67. British Film Institute/National Film Archive
page 68. WN
page 69. HG
page 70. WN
page 71. HG
page 74. CB
page 75. WN
page 76. HG
page 77 WN (courtesy Eva Reichmann)
page 78. Maggs Bros
page 79. HG
page 80. BAL
page 81. BAL / Cheltenham Art Gallery + Museums, Gloucester
page 82. HG
page 83. WN
page 84. WN
page 85. WN
page 86. BAL / Private

Collection
page 87. courtesy Cadogan Hotel, London
page 90. HG
page 92. BAL / Pushkin Museum, Moscow
page 93. HG
page 94. HG
page 95. BAL (Musee Carnavalet, Paris).*
page 97. HG
page 98. HG
page 99. CV / Harlingue
page 100. Popperfoto
page 102-103. BAL / Sheffield City Art Galleries
page 108. The Guardian / Graham Turner
page 106. HG
page 107. CV / Merlin Holland

* ©ADAGP, PARIS AND DACS, LONDON 1997